T0209550

The Learning Organization

Richard Pettinger

- ■ Fast track route to understanding the opportunities and consequences of engaging in organization and individual development as a core business strategy

- ■ Covers the key areas of investment, appraisal, analysis, implementation and evaluation and relates the total approach to long term business and organization viability

- ■ Examples and lessons from some of the world's most successful businesses, including P&O Cross Channel Ferries, Patagonia Inc, Sanyo and Semco, and ideas from the smartest thinkers, including Chris Argyris, Peter Senge and Geert Hofstede

- ■ Includes a glossary of key concepts and a comprehensive resources guide

essential management thinking at your fingertips

ORGANIZATIONS

07.09

First published 2002 by
Capstone Publishing (a Wiley company)
8 Newtec Place
Magdalen Road
Oxford OX4 1RE
United Kingdom
http://www.capstoneideas.com

CIP catalogue records for this book are available from the British Library and the US Library of Congress

ISBN 1-84112-354-4

This book is printed on acid-free paper

Substantial discounts on bulk quantities of Capstone books are available to corporations, professional associations and other organizations. Please contact Capstone for more details on +44 (0)1865 798 623 or (fax) +44 (0)1865 240 941 or (e-mail) info@wiley-capstone.co.uk

Contents

Introduction to ExpressExec

ExpressExec is 3 million words of the latest management thinking compiled into 10 modules. Each module contains 10 individual titles forming a comprehensive resource of current business practice written by leading practitioners in their field. From brand management to balanced scorecard, ExpressExec enables you to grasp the key concepts behind each subject and implement the theory immediately. Each of the 100 titles is available in print and electronic formats.

Through the ExpressExec.com Website you will discover that you can access the complete resource in a number of ways:

» printed books or e-books;
» e-content – PDF or XML (for licensed syndication) adding value to an intranet or Internet site;
» a corporate e-learning/knowledge management solution providing a cost-effective platform for developing skills and sharing knowledge within an organization;
» bespoke delivery – tailored solutions to solve your need.

Why not visit www.expressexec.com and register for free key management briefings, a monthly newsletter and interactive skills checklists. Share your ideas about ExpressExec and your thoughts about business today.

Please contact elound@wiley-capstone.co.uk for more information.

Introduction to the Learning Organization

» The "learning organization" is the generic term given to strategies and initiatives for improving organizational effectiveness.
» The precise nature of the learning process varies between organizations.
» The approach requires expertise and commitment in each of the elements that constitute the total strategic approach.

THE APPROACH

The "learning organization" is the generic term given to strategies and initiatives for improving organizational effectiveness through emphases on developing the capabilities, capacities and qualities of the staff, and on approaches based on behavioral and attitudinal, as well as skills, enhancement.

The approach stems from a corporate commitment to "doing things in our preferred ways." It is an organization-wide strategic process. It is designed in such a way as to integrate all activities with staff collective and individual development and enhancement. It depends for its success on adoption across the board in all departments and functions and by everybody at the place of work.

The approach draws on the direct relationship between the development of staff, and commercial success and service quality advancement. It follows from this that there are roles for change mechanisms, change agents, change catalysts and consultants, as well as key appointments; and this, together with training and development activities, is the driving force by which the organization is taken in preferred directions.

The approach is aimed at changing and forming culture, values, attitudes and beliefs, and developing these in positive and constructive ways.

PROCESS

The precise nature of the process varies between organizations that adopt this form of strategy. In general, the key values and qualities reflect:

» a measure of conformity and the willingness of staff to go down the paths indicated – those who do not wish to do so either come into line and at least conform, or else leave;
» obsession with product and service quality;
» strong commitment to product and service development and enhancement;
» a strong customer orientation;
» universal identity with the organization at large on the part of the staff;

» setting a moral, ethical and value-led example, which is integrated with the commercial or operational drives; and
» taking an active pride in the organization and the work required.

COMPONENT PARTS

The approach requires expertise and commitment in each of the elements that constitute the total strategic approach. These are:

» performance assessment and appraisal;
» problem raising and acknowledgement;
» openness, honesty and trust;
» access to high quality, readily available information;
» inter-group activities and cross-fertilization of ideas; and
» organization assessment and evaluation of the development process (see Summary box 1.1).

SUMMARY BOX 1.1: DEVELOPMENT PROCESSES

It is important to recognize that, for full effectiveness, learning attitudes, approaches and commitment are required whenever the following programs are undertaken:

1 continuous development
2 total quality management
3 business process re-engineering
4 learning cultures
5 organization development (OD)
6 the ascendant organization
7 empowerment strategies.

Many of these programs, when they are implemented within organizations, are led by consultants and other change agents. The development of the behavioral and expertise side is very often neglected when these initiatives are undertaken. Each offers an excellent opportunity; and in those organizations where the particular strategy falls short of full success, this is invariably because insufficient attention has been paid to the staff development side.

CONCLUSIONS

These approaches are important because of the requirements to develop and enhance collective and individual expertise in the pursuit of competitive advantage, and to create the organization culture and climate necessary for the effective management of change. The specific benefit of the approach is that it is strategic, and requires under-standing, consideration and acceptance by top management as they pursue commercial and public service sector goals.

What is the Learning Organization?

» Learning organizations adopt strategic approaches to long-term organizational security, continuity, viability and effectiveness.
» Porter asserts that this is achievable only if a distinctive generic position is first identified, because this influences and informs every subsequent decision. This involves cost leadership, focus and differentiation.
» The strategic perspective may also be viewed from the point of view of groups and individuals within the organization.
» Long-term corporate responsibility requires attention to all aspects of organization and individual development.
» The acronym BASKET defines collective and individual needs.
» Administration must ensure that procedures, appraisal, needs analyses, monitoring, review and evaluation remain current and effective, and contribute to the targeting, development and enhancement of expertise.

Learning organizations adopt strategic approaches to long-term organizational security, continuity, viability, effectiveness – and therefore profitability – that integrates:

» *what* is done and *why* – business and organizational policy, direction, purpose and priorities;

with

» *how* it is done – the specific attention to the staff who have to implement it, and upon whose efforts depends continuing success or failure.

The key, therefore, lies in understanding how the *what*, *why* and *how* are integrated successfully.

STRATEGIC INTEGRATION

Porter, in his book *Competitive Strategy* (Free Press, 1980), defines strategy as

"the series and pattern of decisions that design, shape and inform corporate purpose and direction in order to ensure long-term future and direction."

Porter asserts that this is achievable only if a distinctive generic position is first identified, because this influences and informs every subsequent decision. These positions are:

» cost leadership
» focus
» differentiation.

Cost leadership

This is the drive to be the lowest cost operator in the field. This enables the absolute ability to compete on price where necessary. Where this is not necessary, higher levels of profit and output are achieved in both absolute terms, and also in relation to competitors. Cost leadership requires investment in state of the art production and service technology, and in developing the expertise that its effective operation requires. Organizations that seek cost leadership are lean in form with small hierarchies, large spans of control and operative autonomy; and these approaches therefore address each of these elements.

Focus

This means concentrating on a niche and taking steps to be indispensable. The purpose is to establish a long-term concentrated relationship with specific customers, based on product and service confidence, high levels of quality, utter reliability and the ability to produce and deliver volumes of products and services to order. Investment is necessary in staff expertise and commitment; a part of this is likely to include creativity, problem-solving and attitudes of flexibility and responsiveness.

Differentiation

This means offering homogeneous products on the basis of creating a strong image or identity. Investment is required in marketing, advertising, brand development, strength and loyalty, and outlets and distribution. Investment is required in customer service and management; market-led attitudes; and the capability and willingness to respond to complaints and other failings.

KEY POINTS

Cost leadership, focus and differentiation each require, too, specific attention to skills, knowledge, expertise and technological proficiency development in order to maximize and optimize staff and equipment output over sustained periods of time. The following should be noted.

» Maintaining cost leadership in any sector is dependent on long-term maximization of return on investments from all resources, and this includes continued high levels of attention to staff development.

> » Focus requires investment in fully flexible working, multi-skilling, as well as attitude and behavior development, so that the technology, specialization and output can be geared to any potential customer in the sector.

INDIVIDUALS AND GROUPS IN THE ORGANIZATION

The strategic perspective may also be viewed from the point of view of groups and individuals within the organization.

With regard to *cost advantage*, concentration on maximizing product, service and output develops individual skills and knowledge, and reinforces attitudes and behavior. This enhances individual and collective employability. It develops broader knowledge of the particular organization and its sector. It is also likely to identify potential and opportunities for the future.

Focus concentrates on specific individual and collective skills and knowledge when required. This, in turn, creates greater involvement and participation, and often leads to employee-led business and organization development initiatives. A high degree of loyalty, commitment and motivation is generated where this is the case.

With regard to *differentiation*, employees differentiate themselves through activities undertaken, and experience and qualifications gained and held. This also reinforces employee customer and client perceptions and an understanding of expertise, commitment and confidence – everyone prefers to deal with those who are demonstrably capable and qualified. This, in turn, develops and reinforces positive attitudes and behavior.

Organizations that differentiate themselves through concentrating on employee development also gain reputations for being good employers. Staff are attracted because of the training, development and enhancement on offer, and the opportunities for variety and interest that this is understood to bring.

However, the broader context must still be right. This, above all, means offering the opportunity to put into practice what has been learned and to develop the new skills, knowledge and technological proficiency into expertise. Organizations fall down on this when:

» staff are developed in particular skills and expertise and then have to wait to put it into practice, causing frustration;
» staff are put through particular qualifications without the required professional or occupational support; or
» staff are offered opportunities which are not then delivered.

This last issue is an enduring problem in such occupations as civil engineering, construction management, architecture and other professional services where individuals arrive at work with university qualifications, only to be told that they have now to serve extended periods of time before being given measures of independence and autonomy.

Each of these three problems can be overcome provided that the learning approach is structured to harmonize the needs of individuals with those of the organization.

RAISING EXPECTATIONS

There is nothing overtly wrong with raising peoples' expectations. Most prefer to work in an environment where they are to be well rewarded in return for high levels of expertise and quality of work and output. However, problems always arise when unreal and unachievable expectations are raised.

Many organizations do this - misguidedly - with the best will in the world. They give clear perceptions in job advertisements and recruitment literature of excellent opportunities just to make themselves attractive to well qualified potential staff. This must then be delivered. If it is not, it becomes known and believed to be purely expedient and those caught up in this way quickly move on.

LONG-TERM CORPORATE RESPONSIBILITY

This requires attention to all aspects of organization and individual development. It means creating the required environment and culture, and ensuring that the desired standards of attitudes and behavior, as well as performance, are universally understood and capable of acceptance. It is necessary to attend to at least these two aspects of development:

» *professional*: in which those who hold distinctive expertise and high levels of qualification have the opportunity to develop all aspects of their knowledge, skill and practice; and
» *occupational*: in which everyone has the opportunity to develop their job, and the skills, knowledge and qualities required in ways that enhance their own value, expertise and employability (see Summary box 2.1).

SUMMARY BOX 2.1: EMPLOYABILITY

The term "employability" was defined by Rosabeth Moss Kanter (1985) to explain the combination of professional, occupational and personal added value that learning activities generated.

Kanter defined it as a key form of corporate responsibility. It requires understanding and accepting the view that individual and collective development are essential elements in ensuring long-term, enduring, collective and individual success and effectiveness; and that these are necessary whether staff are going to remain with the organization or move on elsewhere. This has often been an organizational, cultural and perceptual sticking point, and has consequently led to resistance. However, Kanter counters this by making clear that organizations who buy in staff and expertise from elsewhere themselves expect certain levels of aptitude and expertise.

Source: Kanter, R.M. (1985) *The Change Masters*. The Free Press, New York.

Occupational development also includes attention to flexible working practices, multi-skilling, and capability in a wide variety of tasks and activities. It implies the development of attitudes of commitment and loyalty:

» the development of the skills, qualities and expertise required by the *organization*, and the ways in which these are to be applied; and

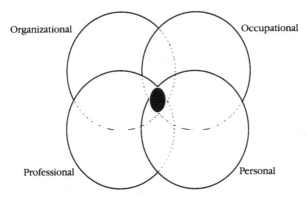

Fig. 2.1 The personal, occupational, organizational, professional mix. Long-term, collective and individual satisfaction is greatest when each of these is covered. The following shortcomings are apparent when the emphases are wrong. *Organizational* – concentration on organizational aspects reduces wider employability and is effective only so long as absolute security of tenure is guaranteed. *Occupational* – this develops current expertise, but is likely to be restrictive when changes are required. *Professional* – concentration on professional development may mean that the individual is effectively being sponsored as a professional, as distinct from professional/organizational operator. *Personal* – over-attention to personal development effectively means that the organization is sponsoring individual preferences.

» consideration of individuals' *personal* preferences and wants, as well as needs (see Fig. 2.1).

BASKET

The acronym BASKET is used to define the collective and individual need to attend to the following elements.

» *Behavior*: attending to the required standards of behavior and ensuring that staff conform to these.
» *Attitudes*: engendering the desired and required attitudes and individual and collective values as a key to culture development.

» *Skills*: attention to the skills, development and enhancement both for the present and future.
» *Knowledge*: developing general, organizational and environmental knowledge, as well as that specifically required for particular jobs and occupations.
» *Expertise*: developing all-round capability in product and service delivery and quality; and including attention to suppliers, customers, financial interests and the community.
» *Technological proficiency*: so that returns on investment on specific items of equipment are maximized.

Each area is required over the medium to long term because of the need to pay attention to developing and reinforcing the *how* – behavior and attitudes – in which the others are to be applied. All development activities must have contextual applications, as well as enhancing total capability and expertise.

PROCESSES AND PRACTICES

Learning organizations require the presence and application of the following:

» collective and individual training needs analyses underpinned by management, supervisory and individual capability in assessing and defining the present and projected activities and requirements;
» performance appraisal systems related directly to implementing and developing core training and enhancement programs – including induction, initial and continuing job training, attention to health and safety, and labor relations procedures and practices;
» capacity for project work and secondments, quality circles, work improvement groups and other aspects of quality assurance;
» developing capability and willingness in problem-solving and the addressing of operational difficulties and blockages;
» developing expertise and willingness in mentoring, coaching and counseling; and
» developing collective and individual expertise in monitoring, review and evaluation – and this includes developing the institutional and

individual capability and willingness to acknowledge when, where and why things have gone wrong.

ORGANIZATIONAL AND ATTITUDINAL STRUCTURING

Corporate and collective attitudes may be viewed as follows (see Fig. 2.2).

» *Low-value*. The best that can be expected is that individuals take responsibility for their own development and do their best outside the constraints of the organization.
» *Ad hoc*. Individual quality is high but unstructured; and again this requires people to devise and implement a strategic and continuous approach to their own development.
» *Administrative*. This can be extremely effective provided that priority is given to analyzing collective and individual needs, booking

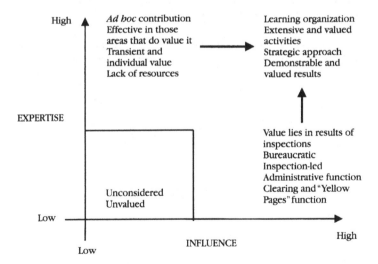

Fig. 2.2   The balance of expertise and influence in organization training functions.

events, following up and providing the procedures and processes for monitoring, review and evaluation.

» *High-value/high-influence*. This means that the strategic position is assured, resourced and capable of full integration.

CONCLUSIONS

To be effective, any "learning organization" approaches must reflect the actual levels of investment and corporate willingness present. If requirements and the present strategic position are out of balance, one or the other has to be remedied.

The approach requires continuous investment and priority in expertise and administration so that institutional delivery and support remain of the highest possible quality. It is also necessary to ensure that everything that is carried out clearly contributes to business production and service performance.

Administration must ensure that procedures, appraisal, needs analyses, monitoring, review and evaluation remain current and effective, and contribute to the targeting, development and enhancement of expertise.

This strategy therefore requires that every element be attended to in the same way as product and service *performance*, supplier and customer management, and attending to the financial returns required.

03

Evolution of the
Learning Organization

» The evolution of learning organizations is studied here under the headings:
  - Cadbury
  - The Hawthorne studies
  - The Tavistock studies
  - Rensis Likert
  - Learning organization research
  - The Japanese experience
  - McKinsey: in search of excellence.

There is no definitive history of learning organizations. However, it is possible to draw specific lessons from particular companies and organizations from different parts of the world as a basis for understanding the prerequisites and requirements for success, and the relationship between the staff-centered approach and the long-term organizational performance.

CADBURY

The Cadbury family who pioneered and built up the chocolate and cocoa industries in the UK in the nineteenth century came from a strong religious tradition (they were Quakers). Determined to be both profitable and ethical, they sought to ensure certain standards of living and quality of life for those who worked for them. They built factories and housing for their staff at a model industrial village at Bourneville on the edge of the city of Birmingham. The village included housing and sanitation, green spaces, schools for the children, and company shops that sold food of a good quality. The purpose was to ensure that the staff were kept fit, healthy and motivated to work in the chocolate factories, producing good quality products; and to ensure both inherent loyalty, and the provision of work for the next generation. Other Quaker foundations operated along similar lines – for example, the Fry and Terry companies that also produced chocolate.

Alongside this however, many employers continued to treat their staff very harshly, keeping them in bad conditions, underpaying them and using fear as the driving force. Almost without exception, these organizations have ceased to exist whereas Cadbury, Fry and Terry continue to trade profitably today, and Cadbury is a major international confectionery and soft drinks company. The work of the company is important as one of the most enduring early industrial examples of the relationship between concern for staff and commercial permanence, profitability and success.

THE HAWTHORNE STUDIES

Pioneering work in human relations was carried out at the Western Electric Company, Chicago, USA over the period 1924–36. Originally designed to draw conclusions between the working environment and work output, these studies finished as major investigations into work groups, social factors and employee attitudes and values, and the effect of these at places of work.

The Hawthorne works of Western Electric Company employed over 30,000 people at the time, making telephone and other electrical equipment. Elton Mayo, Professor of Industrial Research at Harvard University, was called in to advise the company because there was both poor productivity and a high level of employee dissatisfaction.

The first of the experiments was based on the hypothesis that productivity would improve if working conditions were enhanced.

» The first stage was improvement of the lighting for a group of female workers; to give a measure of validity to the results, a control group was established whose lighting was to remain constant. However, the output of both groups improved, and continued to improve, whether the lighting was increased or decreased.
» The second stage extended the experiments to include rest pauses, variations in starting and finishing times and in the timing and length of meal breaks. At each stage, the output of both groups rose until the point at which the women in the experimental group complained that they had too many breaks, and that their work rhythm was being disrupted.
» The third stage was a major attitude survey of over 20,000 of the company's employees. This was conducted over the period 1928–30.
» The fourth and final stage consisted of in-depth observation of both the informal and formal working groups in 1932.

All the threads were then drawn together and resulted in the commencement of staff counseling schemes and other related activities based on the overall conclusions drawn by Mayo and the company. The conclusions were as follows.

1 Individuals need to be given importance and value in their own right, and must also be seen as group or team members.
2 The need to belong at the place of work is of fundamental importance, as critical as both pay and rewards, and working conditions, as a factor in motivation and consistency of work.

3 Formal and informal structures exist, and the informal (especially the staff ability to make a positive contribution whatever their position in the organization) is extremely strong.
4 People respond positively to active involvement at work.

What started out as a survey of the working environment finished as the first major piece of research on attitudes and values prevalent among those drawn together into working situations. These studies were the first to place importance and value on the human side of enterprise and to establish concepts of groups, behavior, personal value, respect and identity in operational situations.

THE TAVISTOCK STUDIES

The concept of the "socio-technical" workplace system was proposed as the result of studies carried out by the Tavistock Institute of Human Relations in the UK during the 1940s, 1950s and 1960s. The work was conducted in a variety of situations including coal mines, cotton mills and prisons.

The socio-technical definition was arrived at because the researchers found that it was not enough to regard work methods as purely functional or operational. The organization and autonomy of the work group itself had to be considered as part of the design of activities to be carried out. If this was disturbed, there was an increase in disputes, grievances, absenteeism and arguments over pay. It was consequently necessary to address both the social and technical or operational aspects if effective work methods were to be devised.

Other findings and conclusions should be noted.

1 The autonomy of the work group and its self-identity is of critical importance. If this is disturbed, by intrusive supervision, technological or operational change, this again leads to increases in disputes and absenteeism if it is not positively managed.
2 There was found to be a clear relationship between the social effectiveness of the group and its work output. As far as work performance was concerned, groups and individuals took a high degree of pride and satisfaction in task achievement and in having the ability to be involved in the whole operation, rather than just a

part of it. An ideal size of work group was defined (consisting of eight persons). There were also found to be high levels of willingness to cooperate on the part of operatives provided that the environment, approach and managerial style were also satisfactory.

The main contribution of the Tavistock studies is to identify the need for all work, work patterns and methods to meet social and psychological needs, as well as those related to task excellence. It also reinforces ideas and motivation that relate to job enrichment and enlargement; to the provision of a quality working environment; and to the importance of effective supervision.

RENSIS LIKERT

Likert's contribution to this approach arose from his studies of high performing managers – managers and supervisors who achieved high levels of productivity, low levels of cost and high levels of employee motivation, participation and involvement at their places of work.

Likert's work demonstrated a correlation between this success, and the style and structure of the work groups that they created. The group's achieved not only high levels of economic output, and therefore wages and salaries, but were also heavily involved in group maintenance activities, and the design and definition of work patterns. At their most effective, they were underpinned by a supportive style of supervision and the generation of a sense of personal value and respect, importance and esteem in belonging to the group itself.

In his book *New Patterns of Management* (McGraw-Hill, 1961), Likert identified four styles or systems of management, and his model evolved into "System 4."

» *System 1 - Exploitative Authoritative*. Power and direction come from the top downwards and there is no participation, consultation or involvement on the part of the workforce. Workforce compliance is based on fear. Unfavorable attitudes are generated, there is little confidence and trust, and low levels of motivation and commitment exist. There are thus no behavioral incentives to do anything but the bare minimum.

» *System 2 – Benevolent Authoritative*. This is similar to System 1, but it allows some upward opportunity for consultation and participation in some areas. Again, attitudes tend to be generally unfavorable. Confidence, trust and communication are also at low levels. In both Systems 1 and 2, productivity may be high over the short run when targets can be achieved by a combination of coercion, bonus and overtime payments. However, both productivity and earnings are demonstrably low over the long run, and there is also high absenteeism and labor turnover.

» *System 3 – Consultative*. Aims and objectives are set after discussion and consultation with subordinates, communication is two-way, and teamwork is encouraged, at least in some areas. Attitudes towards both superiors and the organization tend to be favorable, especially when the organization is working steadily. Productivity tends to be higher, absenteeism and turnover lower. There is also demonstrable reduction in scrap, improvement in product quality, reduction in customer and client complaints, reduction in overall operational costs, and higher levels of earning on the part of the workforce.

» *System 4 – Participative*. Three elements are required for long-term success – the use by the manager of the principle of supportive relationships throughout the work group; the use of group decision-making and collective methods of supervision; and finally the setting of high performance and very ambitious goals for the department and also for the organization overall (see Fig. 3.1).

Likert's preferred system was System 4. To be fully effective and internalized over the long term, the approach required integrating policies, decisions, business and leadership strategies, skills and behavior with collective and individual development. Loyalties, attitudes, motivations and expertise all depended on the overall approach to management and supervision adopted; this reflected the general internal state, climate and health of the organization. Finally, it was necessary to ensure that attention to high levels of participation and involvement resulted in effective product and service delivery, and attention to

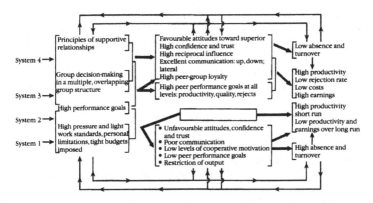

Fig. 3.1 System 4. The purpose is to demonstrate the interrelationship and interaction of the variables defined and present a spectrum of organization and management performance levels (Likert, 1961, with permission).

productivity levels, cost efficiency, and organizational profitability and effectiveness.

LEARNING ORGANIZATION RESEARCH

At the same time as Likert's research, attempts were being made to define the relationship between strategic initiatives in organization and employee development. The research was carried out by Chris Argyris of Harvard Business School; and this was subsequently reinforced during the 1990s by Peter Senge of Massachusetts Institute of Technology (see Chapter 9).

Argyris' contribution arose from research related to staff motivation, carried out at large and highly structured organizations. The overall conclusion was that, because of the pressures and constraints imposed by hierarchies, roles, regulations and tight job descriptions, there was a clear tendency to demotivation on the part of high achievers and capable, excellent and committed performers who found themselves in these circumstances. It was therefore necessary to harmonize individual, collective and organization development so that, as one benefited, so did each of the others. The approach also had the additional benefit of collective corporate recognition of the structural constraints – and these could then be removed.

Senge approached the issue by developing and integrating the related elements of:

» systems thinking rather than fragmentary thinking;
» personal mastery rather than passive responsiveness;
» developing new mental models rather than passively accepting preconceived limitations;
» shared vision rather than fragmented, and often diverse, individual pursuits; and
» team learning in addition to individual development.

Each of these acts as a counter to the rigidity of organization hierarchies and ranks, and provides both a strategic and structural basis for individual, collective and organization learning and development.

THE JAPANESE EXPERIENCE

When Japanese manufacturing organizations first began to export large volumes of products to Western Europe and North America, they quickly developed a reputation for "piling it high, selling it cheap"; and in some cases, this led to accusations of product dumping and market flooding. The goods quickly came to be known and perceived to be cheap and of low value and quality.

In the 1960s, there was a collective attempt by the major organizations to transform this. For example, Sony began to aim their electronic goods at perceived high-quality and high-value niche markets in which they were able to charge premium prices; while Honda and Suzuki competed with Western motorcycle manufacturers on the basis of reliability, durability and consequent enduring-value products (even if these were not as fashionable or distinctive as the Harley Davidson, Triumph, Norton, Villiers or BMW brands).

In the 1970s, Nissan opened manufacturing operations in the West, first in the USA at Smyrna, Tennessee, and later at Washington, Tyne and Wear, UK. The approach transformed the total strategic attitude to manufacturing operations (see Summary box 3.1).

SUMMARY BOX 3.1: NISSAN

Nissan chose locations in areas of high structural unemployment where traditional industries and occupational patterns had collapsed. The company went into the community on a premise of corporate citizenship and enduring value. The long-term stated strategic aims were to provide enduring high quality, value, and lifetime employment. This was designed on the following basis.

1 There were to be high levels of investment in production technology.

2 There were to be high levels of investment in induction, initial and enduring job training. The company expenditure on this in the early 1980s amounted to $16,000 per employee before production lines were switched on; and was reinforced by a continued spend of $8000 per employee, per annum.

3 There was to be trade union recognition based on single-union no-strike deals. In return for their being no constitution for industrial action and collective grievances, the company would design and develop the organization so that there was no possibility of these arising.

4 The company would pay top wages and salaries for the sector, and provide enhanced terms and conditions of employment relating especially to job, occupation and expertise security – in return for fully flexible working practices and the absence of demarcation lines and restraints of trade.

5 The company would institutionalize job rotation and enhancement, provide full equality of opportunity for all, and pay for all off-the-job training and development activities.

MCKINSEY: IN SEARCH OF EXCELLENCE

The genesis of the work that subsequently grew into the management concept of "excellence" was a review carried out in the latter part of the 1970s by McKinsey, the US management consulting firm, of its thinking and approach to business strategy and organizational effectiveness. This review was founded in dissatisfaction with conventional approaches to these matters, and the inability to explain why some organizations were effective while others were not.

In all, 62 organizations were studied. They were drawn from all sectors of US industry and commerce, and included many global firms (e.g. Boeing, McDonald's, Hewlett Packard, 3M). The approach adopted was to study organizations and managers of known and perceived high reputation and/or high performance and to try to isolate the qualities and characteristics that made them so. Those working on the study also identified the attributes that they felt ought to be present in such organizations and persons. The characteristics were:

» leadership and management vision, energy, dynamism and positivism;
» the closeness of the relationship between the organization, its customers and clients;
» staff commitment, motivation, ability, training and development;
» management and supervision levels, hierarchies and chains of command, and their purpose of servicing frontline activities;
» the nature, definition and capability in core business activities;
» attitudes to innovation and improvement, and updating working practices, staff abilities, technology, customer response times and methods;
» receptiveness to ideas and influences from both within, and outside, the organization; and
» the bias towards action, rather than procedure and process.

The studies came to two key conclusions: the essential nature of organization culture, and the importance of macro organizational analysis.

The essential nature of organization culture

In the organizations studied this was:

» a belief in being the best;
» a belief in the importance of staff and individuals for their intrinsic value, as well as their contribution to organization performance;
» a belief in, and obsession with, quality and service;

» a belief that organization members should innovate and have their creative capacities harnessed;

» a belief in the continuous cycle of collective and individual development; and

» a recognition that there is always room for improvement.

The importance of macro organizational analysis

In the organizations studied, this was dependent upon the strength and style of leadership – the drive, determination, core values and strategic vision necessary to make profitable the organization's activities. This was underpinned through overt and perceived values – those issues that managers concern themselves with, those matters on which they actually spend resources, and those people with whom they spend time. It is therefore a combination of both what is done and also how it is done. Messages are given off by this to the rest of the organization. Above all, those in leadership and other positions of responsibility express the true organizational value through the means by which they conduct themselves in all their activities.

CONCLUSIONS

Each of the above contribute to the construction of frameworks that encompass all aspects and activities at corporate, departmental, divisional, team, group and individual levels. Each indicates the range of benefits to be realized provided that the human, as well as operational, side of activities is given strategic attention.

1 Organizations gain a high level of commitment, a strong sense of collective identity and purpose that rise above any divergent individual aims and objectives.

2 Organizations set their own agenda, style and values, rather than allowing these to be manipulated or to decline through a collective lack of concern.

3 Organizations promote understanding, effective communications and continuing high levels of motivation; and provide harmony between normally, or traditionally, divergent business and sectoral or functional interests.

4 Organizations generate opportunities for behavioral, structural and functional development on the part of all concerned. It is enhanced

by the generation of a creative and positive environment for approaches to, and solutions of, problems and blockages.

The techniques indicated above work effectively only where there is full corporate commitment. It is, above all, a business and managerial philosophy. It is not an adjunct or set of activities to be picked up and put down. It enhances cultures and beliefs, as well as profitable and effective performance.

KEY LEARNING POINTS

» Universal identification of attention to staff management and development is a prerequisite for long-term success, effectiveness and viability.

» There are specific lessons from each example of the need for staff development.

» The nature of the lessons is enduring – both the beginnings in previous times, as well as the universality of the conclusion from whichever point of view organizations are studied.

» There is a requirement for a high, distinctive, ethical standpoint.

» There is a relationship between the source of each of the lessons and enduring profitability and effectiveness.

04

The E-Dimension of Learning Organizations

» The e-dimension of learning organizations is discussed here under the headings:
  - The support function
  - The primary function
  - Other uses.
» Best-practice case: Schlumberger SA

The e-dimension of learning organizations has a major contribution to make in the general areas of openness of information, and quality and integrity of communications, as well as providing specific support for learning and development opportunities and activities, and ready access to databases and libraries.

The initial key to effective use of the e-dimension consists of ensuring that everyone has as much access as required, the ability to use the technology effectively, and additional general familiarity that enables the successful development of capability as more sources and opportunities become apparent. Each of these elements constitutes collective development needs. They are increasingly likely to become a part of core training and development programs.

THE SUPPORT FUNCTION

The priority use of the World Wide Web in learning organizations is the provision of structured learning and support materials that can be accessed at the convenience of employees wherever they happen to be located. To be fully effective, the following conditions apply.

» The Web is for support of the main effort and not a substitute for it. Whatever is provided on the Web must have tutor, trainer, facilitator, mentor, coach and counselor support. It must be reinforced by the standards of physical and professional support provided with all other effective organization and employment development activities.

» Conducted in isolation, value is lost. It becomes known, believed and perceived, above all, as a cheap alternative to doing the job properly. It becomes something that people *can* access at any time, but because it is unstructured and unsupported, they never actually *do so*. It quickly becomes known as a low-value substitute for perceived high-quality activities.

» This is also the case where Web-based structured programs are provided. For example, there may be an overtly structured series of progressive exercises, questions and problems through which people are required to work. Nevertheless if:

   » the program produces a limited range of answers according to the input of the student or employee;

» or there is no possibility of discussing or debating either progress or outcomes on a face-to-face basis;

» or if there is no rationale or debrief available on overall performance;

then the value is lost. If employees are sufficiently interested in their own advancement and development, then providers of this particular approach must support it in expected and anticipated ways.

» The Web material must be convenient to access. It must be a substitute or alternative that is known, believed and perceived to be a positive addition to the total range of development materials and opportunities available. If this provision is understood to be inadequate, it will not be used. People will simply revert to more traditional and understood ways of developing their skills, knowledge and expertise, reverting to books, university and college courses and project work.

THE PRIMARY FUNCTION

As an organization and employee development tool, Web-based and computer-based training are more suited to some functions than others.

Simulators

Simulators are essential for initial job training in extreme working environments – for example, healthcare, military and civil aviation. The final test of capability must always be carrying out the job for real, normally initially under supervision. However, computer-based training equipment is universally used in these sectors and occupations to ensure that those who are to use the equipment during the course of their work can first become proficient and familiar with it in a safe environment.

Simulations

Simulations give the opportunity for modeling, projecting and forecasting. They are essential tools in the development of evidence-based practice in which the connection is made between academic and pioneering research, and likely and possible outcomes of particular studies on activities, professions and occupations. Simulations are essential in trying to predict the outcomes of specific medical procedures and drug and pharmaceutical usage, and are normally a precursor to trying them out on a study group of animals, and then humans.

Simulations are also extremely valuable as teaching and demonstration aids, as follows.

» By *architects*, in designing and projecting on-screen mock-ups of how their proposed design might look once built.
» By *archeologists*, in trying to give an impression of how buildings, towns and cities might have looked in the past.
» In *medicine and nursing*, by demonstrating the flow of blood, different reactions within the body, and how particular parts of the body function.
» By *historians*, as an aid to studying and evaluating population movements, military matters, changes in social and religious behavior, the rise and fall of particular civilizations.
» By *sociologists*, as a part of trying to predict movements in society and assessing likely impacts; and in analyzing and understanding the causes and effects of past movements.
» In *town and country planning*, by producing complex simulations to try to project the effects of particular projects and ventures on social and community behavior and capability.
» In *organization management*, by trying to predict the effect of particular decisions, initiatives and proposals; and in the modeling of internal management initiatives – for example, "What if?" approaches to pay rises, restructuring, redeployment and entry into new markets.

Other modeling, extrapolation and forecasting

These are critical and universal organizational, occupational and professional activities that require the following conditions.

» Opportunities for individual and collective development are integrated with these operations.
» Individuals on development paths are given the opportunity to produce their own analyses and explanations, without penalty and with the support of mentors, coaches and counselors (see Chapter 6)

so that their lines of assessment and reasoning are developed. This can be applied to sales, production and market forecasts, human resource management and staff planning, new product and service development and to the supply side also.

Project planning

This too is a more or less universal activity. Again, the approach requires the creation of non-adversarial and supportive conditions if it is to be effective. Those on development paths are guided through processes at each stage. They are allowed (indeed, in many cases required) to present their proposals to those with executive decision-making responsibility. The proposals are then analyzed and evaluated; and inevitably criticized.

The overall climate has therefore to be right if it is to be effective. Everyone involved must be supportive. Where mistakes have clearly been made or gaps are apparent, time must be taken in debriefing, understanding and explaining this.

Overtly, this is clearly more time consuming and adds to pressures on busy executives. The approach taken has therefore to be capable of understanding, acceptance and internalization, as well as designed to fit into timescales, schedules and deadlines (see Summary box 4.1).

SUMMARY BOX 4.1: TIME MANAGEMENT

Effective time management in learning organizations requires acceptance that:

» those on development paths take longer to produce results than do experts;
» mentoring, coaching and counseling require a time priority; and
» debrief on particular activities – computer-based or not – require adequate time allowances.

More generally, effectiveness depends on understanding that:

» busy executives taking decisions at a rush is not necessarily more effective than a considered approach;

» the requirements that take more time may enable opportunities, problems and issues to be identified that might not be apparent in more traditional approaches until too late; and

» if it is necessary to gain full advance compliance of all concerned, a part of this time can be used to gain positive understanding and acceptance.

It is also necessary to remember that lessons learned in these ways are far more likely to be remembered than those that are simply delivered one way. This is especially the case with computer-based training where, because there is no positive debate or interaction with the machine, people will simply work through the program and then leave it. This form of debrief reinforces both the effectiveness of the e-dimension, and also more general positive attitudes.

OTHER USES

The e-dimension gives plenty of scope for e-mail and other non face-to-face tutorials, appraisals, coaching and guidance. For each, there are clear opportunities as a support function and limitations as a primary element. The main problems are the generation of a perceived loss of value and direct and positive support if these become the primary element of each of these activities. Tutorials require the opportunity to discuss and debate, and the e-dimension must support this.

Performance appraisal cannot be truly participative and involving if it is conducted without face-to-face support. The exercise is certain to become a paperwork or screen exercise unless the elements raised by each can then be thrashed out.

Chat-rooms

Provided that these support the main initiatives, they enable wider debate and discussion of development issues and related matters than would otherwise be the case.

This occurs for example, where off-the-job courses are provided for different groups of staff, at different times and locations. Chat-rooms enable those from the different groups to debate and discuss "virtually" where the face-to-face would not be possible (this is also true of video- and teleconferencing). To be fully effective, the approach requires expert and committed facilitator/tutor support.

Trial and error

Safeguards need to be built into the software so that, whatever the employees do as they are learning, they cannot inflict irreparable damage. Properly supported, again, lessons learned are likely to be retained.

Research and development

This can be both in support of particular organization activities and priorities, as well as in the pursuit of funds of increased collective and individual professional and occupational general knowledge, aware- ness and understanding. Organizations do not want, or need, their employees to use up vast amounts of expensive and valuable time and resources *surfing the Net*! On the other hand, scope is required to enable staff to pursue areas of legitimate professional, occupational and organizational interest as the result of their present range of duties.

Professional and occupational development

This is carried out through universal access to professional and specialist libraries and databases. Some of these are free, others require membership as a condition of access. They exist to provide expert and specific bodies of knowledge and understanding on areas of interest and concern. Professional and occupational development provides:

» opportunities for those who work in distant and remote locations away from the main organization (see the best practice case of Schlumberger SA), again provided that these are fully supported by expert and committed staff; and
» trainability and aptitude.

The latter has two main functions: assessing and developing the poten- tial for expertise in the technology itself; and as an aid to illustrating opportunities and alternatives available to particular individuals and groups.

CONCLUSIONS

The keys to effective management of the e-dimension in learning organizations are as follows.

1 There should be corporate responsibility for the entire range of support functions indicated, as well as commitment to providing and developing the technology itself.
2 There must be an understanding that the whole process has to be managed in addition to providing high-quality, current, useful and valuable software.
3 Technological equipment and the broader aspects of the design, development and usage of the e-dimension must be capable of integration with everything else, and enhance the scope for effective activities and project work. It must never become a straightjacket, or a perceived alternative, for doing the job fully and effectively.

Again, as with everything else, these activities and equipment are made available on the basis that they are the best possible approach in the circumstances, and not because they are fashionable, faddish or expedient. Both equipment and access must be made available to everybody who needs it, regardless of rank, status, occupation or length of service.

KEY LEARNING POINTS
» The e-dimension has value as a corporate learning support function.
» The quality of software is important.
» Capability in technological proficiency has to be developed, as well as the use and application of the programs.
» There is a need for physical support of the e-dimension.
» Specific applications have value – simulators, simulations and projections.

» The e-dimension has a use in communicating and delivering organization and employee development activities to those in remote locations.
» There is a need for continuous monitoring, review and evaluation.

BEST PRACTICE CASE: SCHLUMBERGER SA: RIGHT SECOND TIME

Schlumberger SA is a French multinational corporation conducting business in 92 countries. It is a high-technology company that generates the bulk of its income from the oil fields service business – making tools that enable oil companies to find and drill for oil with great precision. It also undertakes drilling, testing and oil well management services, including pumping and design. It acts as an engineering and industrial consultant to all of the major oil companies of the world. It manages databases of investigations and explorations in all parts of the world. It depends extensively on high-quality engineering, geotechnical, geophysical and geological expertise that it draws from the best universities of the European Union, North America and the Far East.

Based in Paris, the company sends these highly expert and well-rewarded engineering staff, geologists, mining specialists and technological operatives all over the world. Their primary functions are:

» to prospect for oil so that contractual arrangements can be entered into with drilling, supplying, refining and distribution companies;
» to advise on the most effective ways of extracting oil and gas from the places where it is found, providing economic analyses, and getting into the locations required; and
» to solve technological and complex problems as and when these arise.

Accordingly, staff are required to work in some of the most remote, forbidding and inaccessible parts of the world. They endure long periods (up to six months without a break) in extremes of climate, often with the most basic sanitation and accommodation facilities. Physical contact with the outside world and the company itself are irregular, and dependent on helicopter access or long and tricky road journeys.

These staff tend to be young (22–40). They are extremely well paid – many earn basic salaries before allowances upwards of $100,000 per annum. They are provided with laptop computers and mobile phones, though the latter are often not useful in particular locations, and it may also not always be possible to charge them up.

Accordingly, the main contact with the outside world is by e-mail. Everything is transmitted and received in this way. Because of the location issues, this is accepted as the best approach all round.

The company has, for many years, engaged in a form of individual and collective development, with the purposes of:

» staff and management development of the next generation of senior executives from among the ranks of the technological and professional staff; and
» medium- to long-term culture change from a paternalistic to task-focussed approach.

The company engaged the University of Edinburgh, Scotland, to provide this. For many years it was quite effective as a staff retainer because it was known, believed and perceived to provide a career path, a "way out of the desert" into head-quarters and regional office functions. The course elements each lasted for one week and took place at excellent hotels located in different parts of the world – Djakarta, Dubai, Paris, New York and Acapulco.

The company proposed to shift large parts of the management development program to the Web. It undertook to provide on-line tutorials, chat-room and other virtual support. At the same time, it was proposed that the hotel-based delivery of the program be reduced.

Both interest and perceived value declined sharply. While the company perceived that those wanting the development would log-on at quiet moments in their working lives, in practice this did not happen. Not everyone had access to printing facilities and so information had to be read from screen. It was also impossible to engage in the forms of discussion necessary for effective skills, knowledge and analytical development.

Most importantly, however, technical, professional and engineering staff perceived a loss of personal value and respect because the luxury hotel accommodation was universally regarded as part of the reward package and the opportunity to enjoy some civilization, as well as being a high-quality learning experience. It was also good to meet up with others and to share experiences, hopes, fears and aspirations.

Faced with a loss of interest and declining morale, the company accordingly revised the Web-based part of the strategy. Course outlines, support materials and some further reading were placed on the Web, but core contact, exercises and assignments were removed. These were returned to the hotel-based seminars, which were reinstated. The chat-room was kept on but it quickly became a more general forum for debate and information exchange.

Tutorials continued to be delivered on a regular basis by e-mail. However, they depended for lasting effectiveness on support by tutors and facilitators when course members gathered together.

The taught part of the program was reinstated in full and developed further. It subsequently became accredited as a full Masters program (MSc) in oil technology and management.

05

The Global Dimension of Learning Organizations

» Learning organization approaches to globalization are discussed here under the following headings:
  - The Japanese
  - The niche
  - Mass production and services
  - Culture.
» Best practice case: Canon Inc.

Wherever in the world organizations operate, they require competitive advantage and enduring effectiveness – in whatever terms they themselves measure these. Learning organizations approach this on the basis that it represents a key source of long-term sustainable competitive advantage, and the capability and willingness to cope with environmental pressures, change, uncertainty and sectoral turbulence. The following distinctive approaches are apparent.

THE JAPANESE

The Japanese approach is to integrate everything into corporate strategy (see also Chapter 3). This means paying attention to all aspects of known, understood and perceived employee requirements – job and work security, pay and rewards, and prospects for advancement. It is driven by fully flexible working and the absence of restrictive practices that still prevail in some sectors in the West, and also in the newly independent states of the former Communist bloc. High and continued levels of investment are committed to the following.

» *Induction and orientation*, including attitude and identity formation and acceptance (see Fig. 5.1). The approach is to establish a position of acceptance during induction and to develop this into the known and understood mutuality of loyalty and interest that accrues with genuine internalization. Some company induction programs (see the best practice case example of Canon) take up to four weeks. They include residential periods so that a social, as well as occupational and professional, cohesion is achieved.

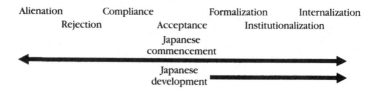

Fig. 5.1   Induction, attitude and identity formation.

» *Initial and continuous job training*, so that present capabilities are shaped and refined in order to be able to carry out work in the ways required; and also to begin to develop any other specific technical or occupational competence required.
» *Extensive core programs*, so that full familiarity with procedures and practices are internalized.

This all then becomes the precursor to both prescribed and agreed professional, technological and occupational development.

THE NICHE

Organizations that produce real and perceived high-quality high-value products, goods and services that are sold at premium prices have to create a distinctive staff culture in support of this. This applies to the following:

» luxury, exclusive and other niche products – e.g. Harley Davidson and Rolls Royce;
» luxury, exclusive and other niche service delivery – e.g. Lillywhites, Harrods;
» exclusive and perceived high-value offerings made by otherwise mainstream suppliers – e.g. Toyota/Lexus, Ford/Jaguar;
» broader niche products and services – e.g. Marks & Spencer, BMW;
» high brand values – e.g. Virgin;
» high-quality professional services – e.g. architecture, project management, accountancy;
» quirks and oddities – e.g. Body Shop; and
» single-site single-location operations – e.g. *haute couture*, exclusive restaurants, executive travel.

Factors common to all these organizations include the following.

1 There are high and distinctive levels of staff training and expertise in product and service knowledge and understanding. Those engaged in this form of activity are required to be prepared to produce unique and customized versions of products and services in response to specific customer demands. Those engaged specifically in service delivery are required to accept that they carry the full weight of the

organization and customer expectations. A wrong move may lose both reputation and also thousands of dollars worth of business.

2 There are high levels of personal, as well as professional, occupational and technical, pride and commitment. Some of this will be instilled at induction; and individuals are likely to come to work at the particular organization with this as a preconception.

3 There is personal, professional and occupational commitment to the organization as an intrinsic interest. Those who work for Harley Davidson, Virgin or BMW are expected to be enthusiasts, as well as extremely professional.

All of this can be achieved only if the organization recognizes the direct relationship between this level of commitment and enduring customer satisfaction leading to continuous flows of business; and is consequently prepared to invest in the organization's standards and collective development required.

MASS PRODUCTION AND SERVICES

The potential for competitive advantage exists also in mass production and standard retail services (see Summary box 5.1).

SUMMARY BOX 5.1: LEARNING ORGANIZATIONS AND MASS MARKETS: EXAMPLES

» **UK retail**: Tesco, the UK supermarket company, doubled its share from 10% to 20% of the UK grocery market as the result of concentrating on initial and continuous accredited staff development alongside network expansion, product range diversification and greater attention to the actual wants of customers.

» **US retail**: Walmart remains the largest supermarket chain in the world by ensuring that there is training and development in autonomy and responsibility for all staff. This is connected to a required internalized positive attitude and sunny disposition on the part of all staff. Customer requirements must always be dealt with on the spot. Consequently, staff are required to know what can be done in order to ensure that business is maintained and developed.

» **Japanese cars**: Nissan undertook a major initiative in support of making production crews directly answerable for quality assurance and customer complaints. Individual cars were numbered as they came off the production line so that any problems could be addressed to the people who actually made them.

CULTURE

As stated above (see Chapter 2), the "learning organization" approach is concerned with attitude and behavior development, as well as expertise. This consists of establishing and assuring collective attitudes and values to which everyone is prepared to subscribe. There are several requisites.

» It requires a high level of corporate and collective integrity so that it is known and understood that attitudes and values are instituted and reinforced in the interests of all.
» It requires a high degree of participation and involvement. This is necessary, especially in terms of access to key members of staff, and the willingness to address and resolve problems and issues through collective and individual development. Also essential is openness, transparency and availability of company information so that everyone understands why particular courses of action are being taken.

It is also necessary to attend to particular social and environmental pressures so that:

» particular restraints can be assessed and addressed; and
» standards can be established that transcend local differences.

This requires specific attention to the following.

» The interaction between the desired culture and the organization structures and systems. Serious misfit between these leads to stress and frustration, and also to customer dissatisfaction and staff demotivation.

» The expectations and aspirations of staff, and the extent to which these are realistic and can be satisfied within the organization. This can become a serious issue when the nature of the organization changes and prevailing expectations can no longer be accommodated.

» Management and supervisory style, and the extent to which those in positions of responsibility have capability, willingness and expertise in the qualities and approaches required.

» The qualities and expertise of different staff groups, and the extent to which this divides their loyalties. Many staff groups have professional or trade union memberships, continuous professional and occupational requirements and career expectations, as well as the requirement to hold down positions and carry out tasks within the particular organization.

» The effect of technology and changes in technology, and the extent to which these impact on the ways in which work is designed, structured and carried out.

» Working customs, traditions and practices, including work divisions, specialization and allocation; and the attitudes and approaches adopted by both organization and staff towards each other.

» The extent to which long-term enduring continuity of employment is feasible; or conversely, the nature of the uncertainty surrounding future prospects of work and employment. This includes the ability to instill degrees of flexibility, the present and desired state of employee and skills development.

» Internal approaches and attitudes to legal and ethical issues indicated; the extent of genuine commitment to equality of opportunity and access for all staff; the known, believed or perceived differences to which different grades of staff have different values placed upon them; absolute standards of dealings with staff, customers, suppliers, communities and distributors.

» The presence of pride and commitment in the organization, its work and reputation.

» Physical and psychological distance between functions, departments, divisions, occupations and the positions in the organization and its hierarchies, departments, divisions and functions (see Summary box 5.2).

SUMMARY BOX 5.2: KAIZEN

Kaizen is a Japanese term referring to the constant progress of humanity and the continuous striving for perfection, and "constant continuous development." It refers to all aspects of organizations – above all, the requirement to develop culture as a precondition of effective product and service performance.

Kaizen requires continuous:

- staff training and development;
- product and service improvement;
- attention to productivity;
- attention to procedures and administration to make each as simple and clear as possible; and
- attention to the whole organization, as well as its parts; and continuous improvement in the integration of the parts into the whole.

The desired result is continued output of high volumes of high-quality products, often at premium prices. This is supported by adaptation and innovation, as well as creativity. This is, in turn, is supported by an absolute commitment to high levels of investment in all aspects of staff development, as well as business performance and maximizing returns on investment in technology. High levels of expectations are placed on staff. High degrees of conformity and internalization are required; and in return for this, high levels of pay and security of employment are offered.

Related to this is *Mu*, or complete openness. This constitutes a refusal to be hidebound by policies, constraints, directions and structures. Requirements include being receptive to ideas, innovations, opportunities and potential; and engendering the qualities of vitality, flexibility, responsiveness and adaptability on a collective, as well as individual, basis. The guiding principle of the company is "to live for a long time" rather than to be "the best airline" or "the best car company." It was this approach that enabled Mitsubishi to transform relatively easily from shipbuilder to car manufacturer.

Purposes and goals are set according to the demands and opportunities of the global environment, rather than preordained and specialized internal strategies – indeed, corporate strategy consists of having the staff, capital, technology and capability to respond to demands and opportunities.

CONCLUSIONS

Setting and maintaining the highest possible standards of individual and collective development, and underpinning these with strong positive attitudes and values, means that the organization is likely to be fundamentally acceptable anywhere in the world where it chooses to conduct its activities. These standards transcend local, cultural, social and religious pressures because they are designed to ensure:

» the principles on which they are based
» the human values present, and
» the wider contribution made

are universally desired, rather than simply meeting local, legal and operational minima.

These elements are of especial value when seeking to establish in new markets and locations, and in attracting high-quality fresh talent. They are key elements in developing high levels of loyalty and commitment, as well as technical, occupational and professional expertise.

KEY LEARNING POINTS

It is important to:

» relate the strategic approach to organizational, environmental and cultural demands as well as business performance;
» set standards that transcend local differences;

- » stress positive attitudes and values;
- » give individuals standards, attitudes and values, as well as capabilities, which are capable of internalization;
- » draw on lessons from everywhere in the world; and specific understanding of the relationship between Japanese approaches and enduring business success; and
- » attend to culture management.

BEST PRACTICE CASE: CANON INC.: TRANSCENDING LOCAL EXPECTATIONS

Canon is a Japanese multinational corporation that manufactures, sells and distributes photographic equipment to industrial and consumer markets. It has two distinctive core product lines.

- » It produces medium- to high-price, high and enduring quality and value cameras for the consumer market. These are distributed through department stores and specialist outlets in 130 countries. In support of this, the company subcontracts the manufacture of branded accessories – e.g. tripods, carrying cases and clothing. It also manufactures specialist editions – e.g. lenses and filters.
- » It also produces high-price, premium-charge, industrial and commercial office photocopying and document reproduction equipment. This is supported with high-charge, high-quality and value, enduring product after-sales servicing, repair and replacement services.

Canon draws a direct relationship between stability, security and satisfaction of the workforce in all of the localities where business is conducted. Pay and terms and conditions of employment are designed to ensure that they are acceptable in absolute terms in return for high levels of commitment, expertise and effort; and sufficiently competitive in local terms to be able to attract staff from elsewhere if required.

Once employed, new staff go through a two-week job- and work-based induction program for factory staff, and a three-week off-site residential sales training period for sales staff. Managerial staff are required to undertake both on-the-job and off-the-job periods of induction, core training, and professional and expertise management development.

Each consists of attitudes, value and behavior formation and cultural immersion, as well as attention to technological and occupational proficiency. This is highly conformist. The company requires distinctive standards and approaches to both manufacturing and sales; and capabilities in product knowledge, human relations management, and problem-solving in managerial staff.

Gambara

Gambara is a work ethic traditionally imbued by Japanese society; it means "don't give up, do your best, be persistent, put in a great effort." This is related to a high concept of service that is widely regarded within the Canon company. Service is regarded as being not only at the customer or immediate interface, but also over the lifetime of the products provided, and for new products and models and their value to the customer. The company works for the good of both staff and the customers; and adopts the view that it functions effectively only when all parts are operating to full effect and capacity, and in harmony with each other.

Manufacturing is based on a combination of flexible working and a structured multi-skilling program so that everyone becomes as fully proficient as possible in short order.

Factory staff engage in job rotation, enhancement and enlargement. They are expected to take an active part in factory improvement groups that address working environment, as well as product quality. Quality assurance and customer and client services management are integrated with production activities.

Sales staff are inducted into a range of pre-designed overall approaches. Especially on the photocopier side, contractual arrangements required, and desired, are clearly stated. These then have to be harmonized with customer and client requirements. Sales staff are regularly rotated in their territories; they are also required to undertake the broadest possible attitude to account management and customer and client liaison.

The company takes the view that a lost or unachieved contract is the beginning of a conversation that is to end when Canon gains the particular organization or individual as a client. Sales staff are consequently required to maintain and record contacts with lost clients, non-clients, potential clients and existing clients. Existing clients are always offered the chance to replace and upgrade their equipment, increasing value and quality of service in return for higher charges.

Both factory and sales staff are supported with product awareness and development seminars. They are required to participate in work improvement and quality improvement groups, some of which take place in locations other than the place of work, and during non-work time.

The attitude is consequently very conformist. The company view is that only by setting these standards can this level and quality of service be maintained and developed. It requires particular levels of commitment from the staff. This is achieved only if attitudes, values and behavior are first learned, then internalized and reinforced.

06

The State of the Art

» The support of top management is required.
» Business development requires that the implementation of strategy and the evaluation of opportunities and potential be institutionalized from the point of view of collective and individual learning, as well as attention to customer and client needs.
» Effective problem-solving is possible only if there is a fundamental corporate openness and honesty, and collective and individual willingness to learn from errors.
» Effective appraisal and analysis depends on a continuous positive relationship between supervisors and subordinates, punctuated with regular formal reviews.
» A strategic view must be taken of the collective present, desired and required staff expertise. It is then essential to decide how the gaps between each are best addressed.
» For groups to remain effective, monitoring and review processes and activities must be developed and become in-built.
» Managing change requires the creation of a collective, positive attitude and receptiveness to change.

Learning organizations require the integration of strategy, direction, purpose, priorities, profitability and effectiveness with continuous collective and individual development. This, it has been argued, ensures a human – as well as occupational – commitment to purpose, leading to personal identity and relationship with the organization. This, in turn, leads to the generation of qualities of loyalty, belonging and pride.

KEY REFERENCES
» Heller, R. (1998) *In Search of European Excellence*. Harper-Collins Business.
» Fowler, A (2000) *New Patterns of Work*. IPD.

No single or prescribed body of knowledge or expertise exists as a basis for enduringly successful learning organizations. However, the following elements are more or less universally present when organizations in all sectors and parts of the world choose this approach.

TOP MANAGEMENT SUPPORT

The support of top management is required, together with full understanding and acceptance at board level and backed by shareholders' representatives (or public service fund holders and providers); strategic acceptance of what is being done, why and how; and the results that are expected and required to accrue. Capital providers are being asked to accept that this is the best path in the circumstances to growth, sustainability, effectiveness and profitability.

BUSINESS DEVELOPMENT

Business development requires that the implementation of strategy and the evaluation of opportunities and potential be institutionalized from the point of view of collective and individual learning, as well as attention to customer and client needs. The reasoning is as follows.

1 There is a direct and integrated relationship between learning, development and performance.

2 Those involved are much more likely to learn and retain lessons in these ways and so bring new awareness and expertise to bear on future activities.

3 A collective commitment is engaged so that opportunities and possibilities are recognized by all. This, it is argued (Peters, 1986), is much more likely to be effective than concentrating responsibility for it in think-tanks or specialist groups.

PROBLEM-SOLVING

Effective problem-solving is possible only if there is a fundamental corporate openness and honesty, and collective and individual willingness to learn from errors (see Summary box 6.1).

SUMMARY BOX 6.1: SUCCESS AND FAILURE – 1

Success and failure are value judgements placed, both individually and collectively, on activities, events, products, services and projects. Learning organizations are especially concerned with:

» why particular activities and events are considered successes and failures, and by whom;

» whether this is a collective, pressurized or valid judgement and the integrity of the line of reasoning that supports it; and

» what can be learned from it, and by whom.

Success should be evaluated in the same way. Many organizations and their managers accept success as it comes along without ever fully evaluating the reasons. This occurs especially where it is as the result of substantial, collective or individual human effort (as well as professional, technological and occupational expertise).

Similarly, failure tends to be judged as "one of those things." In his book *The Fifth Discipline*, C.M. Senge (Century Business, 1998) refers to this as "the enemy is out there." This reflects the need to find external causes and agents to blame rather than accepting active responsibility for one's own destiny and the shortcomings that are certain to occur as a result.

Everything is therefore subject to open and honest scrutiny. This includes the capability to raise problems, issues and concerns without fear or favor; to consider the various options available; and to extrapolate the opportunities and consequences that each brings. This sounds long-winded. It is not, especially when the haphazard nature of many mainstream alternatives are considered (see Summary box 6.2).

SUMMARY BOX 6.2: MAINSTREAM APPROACHES TO PROBLEM-SOLVING

The main alternatives to the "learning" approach are effective and successful where procedures and practices are known, understood and followed, and where time is allowed for sufficient, all-round understanding and information gathering anyway. Otherwise, attention is required to avoid the following:

» expediency, where a problem is solved to get a short-term result despite the long-term consequences;
» the need to demonstrate perceived quick capability to a higher authority;
» the need to solve problems as part of the reason for being – this is especially a problem in human resource and labor relations activities because such functions exist only to solve problems, so they require problems to solve; and
» the direction of top and senior managers in requiring a particular solution to an issue, whether or not this is right.

It does however, require some attention to time management (see Chapter 4) so that there is at least a modicum of capability and capacity for a collective approach even when things are urgent.

PERFORMANCE APPRAISAL AND TRAINING NEEDS ANALYSES

Performance appraisal and training needs analyses are required as a strategic and integrated approach to performance, and to professional, occupational and technological development. Appraisals and analyses are related directly to core training and development requirements; the demands of continuous professional and occupational development; and individual needs and wants. Long-term effectiveness also depends on the corporate willingness to address personal needs and wants, to accept that individuals have active responsibilities for the ways in which their careers and occupations are to progress.

Effective appraisal and analysis depends on a continuous positive relationship between supervisors and subordinates, punctuated with regular formal reviews (ideally every 3-4 months, and certainly with no greater interval than six months between formal reviews). The formal element is never punitive, but rather a scheduled opportunity for both to discuss and agree short- and medium-term strategies for development, and integrating these with workplace demands. The employee then commits to undertaking what is required, and the supervisor to supporting it.

ATTENDING DEVELOPMENT EVENTS

This depends on making available organization and employee development events, both on and off the job, and including projects and secondments, as well as courses and skills development. Once committed to, the required events must be made available. These consist of:

» on-the-job training and project work, and the opportunity to participate in brainstorming, work improvement, quality improvement and location improvement group activities;
» off-the-job events – short courses, secondments and, when required, professional and occupational development through business schools (management development), medical schools (doctors, nurses and other healthcare professions), technical training and workshops (engineering and software occupations), enhanced status and professionalism (all technical, occupational and professional activities), environmental issues (e.g. health and safety, product performance, the introduction of new technology and equipment);
» planned and stated experience so that employees develop their all-round understanding of the totality of the organization, as well as their own capability; and

» specific attention to job enrichment and job enlargement which normally leads to flexibility and variety – and enhances general employability, value and worth, to both the individuals concerned and to the organization.

Whatever events are proposed must be capable of scrutiny and justification from the following points of view.

» There must be a clear and positive contribution to organizational effectiveness, business and opportunities development.
» There must be early opportunities to put newly learned skills, expertise and technological proficiency into action, with or without the physical presence of support.
» There must ultimately be benefits to both organization and individual. Organizations that sponsor their staff through MBA programs are entitled to expect enhanced business and managerial capability. Employees who attend specific occupation and organization demanded events are entitled to expect personal and occupational recognition, as well as contributing to increased organizational effectiveness.

Whatever is put on must be fully supported. The following mechanisms are usually found:

» mentoring, coaching and counseling
» monitoring, review and evaluation.

Mentoring, coaching and counseling

Mentoring, coaching and counseling relationships are engaged in:

» between superiors and subordinates; or
» between experts and those developing expertise; or
» with the purpose of ensuring adequate support through periods of development and enhancement, project work and secondments (see Fig. 6.1).

These relationships are sometimes more generally referred to as partnering or "buddy" systems. Whatever the approach, high levels of responsibility and integrity are required as follows:

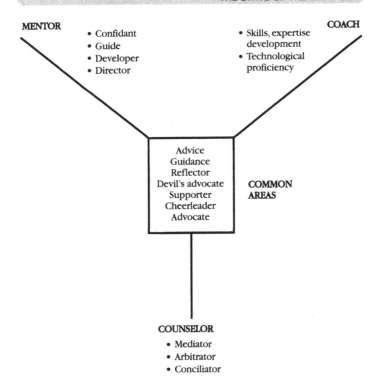

Fig. 6.1 The relationship between mentoring, coaching and counseling.

1 *Mentors* are responsible for support and guidance through all aspects of development, and the potential therefore exists to shape and skew these activities in their interests, and to claim the credit for work success and achievements of those they are mentoring. In some cases, they may also use their protégés as "human shields" – driving forward something that is in their own interests, and hiding behind the protégé if things go wrong.

2 *Protégés/employees* are responsible for carrying out the training, project or secondment and the work attached to it. Employees may

choose projects and mentors that they perceive or understand to be high profile as a means of accelerating their own promotion prospects, or gaining high-profile triumphs. They too may use their mentor as a "human shield" by taking trouble to ensure that everyone knows who is mentoring and nurturing the particular activity, and then publicly blaming them if it does not work out.

Mentor/protégé relationships need to be engaged in on the basis that they are long term. Long-term benefits are certain to accrue to each and open up fresh opportunities. However, they require fundamental foundations of honesty, integrity, trust and mutual value if the benefits are to truly occur.

Employees may also turn to someone as a *coach* to get them over particular problems (see Fig. 6.1). Alongside an open and fully participative environment, there is no reason why anyone should not approach anyone else for help on particular issues. There is plenty of potential for the relationship to develop more fully into that of mentor provided that both wish it, and capability and commitment are present.

Monitoring, review and evaluation

Everything that is done must be the subject of full scrutiny. It is essential to debrief individuals and groups at the point of completion of work tasks and projects. Again, there is a distinctive element of time and priority management – if everyone is to evaluate what has happened and learn from it (this applies to both successes and failures – see Summary box 6.1), then those in senior and responsible positions need to make themselves available for this purpose.

Immediate review should take place also at the end of all off-the-job training and development activities. This should be conducted by employer and employee, as well as the activity provider, facilitator, lecturer, tutor or trainer.

This can then be followed by a more considered view over the ensuing weeks and months. During this period, the state of proficiency in what has been learned begins to become apparent. The individual can then assess personal progress and proficiency. The employer assesses total contribution as the result of the newly acquired skill or quality. This forms a key issue to be discussed at the next performance review.

Ultimate responsibility remains joint. However, those in supervisory or mentoring positions are required to lead, direct and steer; and at different times must be prepared to act as guide, advocate, cheerleader, teacher and sounding board. They must also be prepared to impose and justify discipline, constraints and steerage when matters are getting out of hand, or when employees are carried away with their own enthusiasm, or when staged approaches to projects and problems are clearly indicated.

THE GROW-YOUR-OWN/BUY-IN MIX

A strategic view must be taken of the collective present, desired and required expertise. It is then essential to decide how the gaps between each are best addressed. Because of the integration of collective development and business purpose, especial attention is required when it is determined that the best course of action is to bring in expertise and fresh blood from outside.

All organizations need to be able to do this from time to time. It helps to ensure a fresh flow of general talent and capabilities. Carried out correctly, this complements and enhances the performance of those already present.

It may also be required as an organization "punctuation mark." For example, the employment of a high-profile senior figure who is an expert in their particular field enhances perceptions, as well as the reality, of the importance of the particular area of activity.

Wherever this approach is implemented, bringing in outside expertise must be capable of honest and sustainable justification. Existing staff brought up in a collective culture and climate – who have always been given the first chance to do something – need to be told, and to accept, the reasons why this is not possible in particular cases and circumstances. Organizations that fail to do this on a regular basis quickly dilute the total effort.

New senior and high-profile staff require the same extensive induction and orientation programs referred to in Chapters 3 and 5 so that their distinctive expertise and contribution is quickly harmonized and integrated with existing ways of working.

GROUP AND COLLECTIVE DEVELOPMENT

In terms of the process of establishing, building and developing groups, the following aspects are required.

» *Management and development of tasks and activities*: setting and developing work methods, timescales, resources; addressing problem-solving and blockage management.

» *Management and development of processes*: the use of interpersonal skills and interaction with technology to gain the maximum contribution from each individual; and ensuring as full a flexibility of operation as possible.

» *Managing communications*: between different work groups, disciplines and professions, and within particular work groups; addressing the needs, wants and expectations of particular occupations within work groups; to recognize and manage the potential for conflicts.

» *Managing and developing the individual*: making constructive use of individual differences; ensuring that individual contributions are both valued and of value.

» *Management style*: creating and developing the desired, and required, aspects of environment, behavior and culture; developing the distinctive managerial expertise required to ensure that this is managed and developed.

» *Maintenance management*: ensuring that administration and support services are suitable for the needs of the group; developing these in harmony with product and service culture and behavior, and occupational development.

» *Common aims and objectives*: that are understood, valued and adopted by everyone concerned; these remain the overriding common purpose for being in the situation; they are harmonized with individual and occupational objectives.

» *Group and team spirit*: developing a combination of the shared values, ethics and ethos of the particular group or team and the extent of the positive identity and loyalty that members have to each other, as well as to the tasks in hand and to the overall objectives. Group and team spirit must always be positive; where negative elements exist, these must be addressed as a matter of priority.

For groups to remain effective, monitoring and review processes and activities must be developed and become in-built. They must take the form both of continuous processes and activities, and of regular formal progress meetings. All groups also benefit from external feedback, monitoring and contacts. Such reviews must take account of all elements. All contributions to the overall effectiveness of performance of groups must be addressed. Dysfunction in any of these detracts from the totality of performance, outputs, tasks, purposes and cohesion.

MANAGEMENT DEVELOPMENT

Approaches to management development require assessment of the following.

1 Capability – the presence of skills, qualities and expertise in organization planning, controlling, motivation, work scheduling and setting aims and objectives as required.
2 The ability to plan for present and future, and to integrate collective and individual development with required functional outputs.
3 The ability to measure performance – and this includes the capability to take remedial action (integrating provision for development) where this falls short of desired results.
4 The ability to take evaluative action – including the provision for development – where desired results are achieved (see Summary box 6.3).
5 The ability to communicate effectively and positively with all staff. This is reinforced by a commitment to visibility (managing by walking around) and time must be set aside for this. It reinforces overall style and openness, as well as enabling the early observation and raising of potential problems and issues.
6 The ability to take effective decisions, to communicate these and be able to support and justify them. This requires a standard and well understood process adapted to take account of the following:
    » the need to present decisions and discuss them with those directly concerned and other legitimate interests;
    » the need to gain active understanding even where overall sympathy is not possible (e.g. assigning people to non-preferred tasks); and

» the need to address individual and collective concerns arising as the result of the decision (see Fig. 6.2).

SUMMARY BOX 6.3: SUCCESS AND FAILURE – 2

As stated above, and elsewhere, constant attention is required to measuring performance and assessing success and failure. Of particular concern here is where success is achieved "beyond our wildest dreams." Two responses are possible:

» all-round backslapping, mutual congratulations and celebration of a triumph; and
» all-round backslapping and mutual congratulations, followed immediately by analysis and evaluation of why targets were so low, expectations not raised, and projections so inaccurate.

The objective must be to learn from the points of imperfection even where this level of overt success is apparent.

Willingness

Managers in all circumstances *should* be enthusiastic, committed, ambitious, self-motivated and interested in every aspect of organizational, departmental, collective and individual performance. These qualities are absolute prerequisites. Also required is the absence of personal likes and dislikes. Managers must be prepared and willing to progress all employees as far as they can go. Where it becomes apparent that some individuals are happy just to potter along, they need to be fired up with enthusiasm.

Managers also need to develop specific enthusiasm for performance and behavioral enhancement and development, and a willingness to sell these if required to the staff. The approach is based on enthusiasm and a positive attitude being infectious. So long as this is supported with integrity, openness and capability, managers are entitled to expect positive responses and commitment in return.

Application

The key to understanding the application of learning organization principles in particular departments, divisions and functions lies in

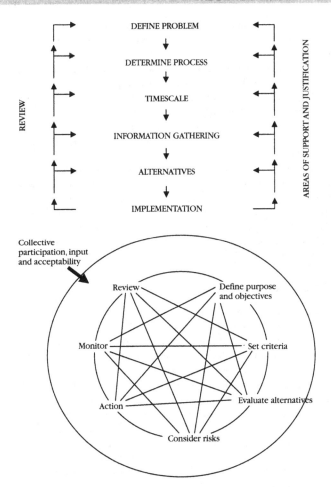

Fig. 6.2 A decision-making model. The purpose is to draw the distinction between the two elements of progression (top) and process (below). The former is a schematic approach; the latter is that from which the former arises, and which refines it into its final format. Effective and successful decision-making requires the confidence that is generated by continued operation of the process.

total managerial knowledge of everything that is required and goes on. This can be fully achieved only by physical presence. This underlines the need for "managing by walking around." It forms the basis for an effective and positive managerial and supervisory style overall, and for any variations which may be required from time to time.

This is both possible and also required in any organization, structure and culture where these approaches are adopted, and is both effective and successful in bureaucratic and hierarchical structures (e.g. Boeing, Airbus, Nissan) as in smaller or more perceived open organizations (e.g. Body Shop, Virgin Group).

Managers also need to be able to vary their approach (some would say their style) according to the nature of the group or individuals with whom they are dealing. Some require prescriptive approaches, others require the opportunity to debate and discuss issues at length. Effective approaches, whether variations in style or not, are only achieved by a full understanding of the work and respect for the positions of the individuals who carry it out.

MANAGING CHANGE

A primary purpose for engaging in these strategies is to ensure that the attitudes, values and behavior are created alongside technological proficiency and occupational skills and expertise, the end result of which is the creation of a collective, positive attitude and receptiveness to change. This is normally engaged as the result initially of ensuring high-quality, regular information about performance, competition, state of markets and product and service lifecycles so that everyone understands why change is required. This provides a platform for developing qualities of versatility, adaptiveness and receptiveness, and to see change as a collective and individual opportunity, rather than as a restraint.

These approaches make it much easier to identify where real resistance to change exists. These are most commonly found as the following.

» Vested interests, lobbies and self-interest groups may have a present vision and influence that is perceived to be threatened by change. The approach requires activities that substitute or replace present influence and interest with that collectively needed for the future;

and which also pays attention to the loss of anticipated career paths (e.g. by substituting variety and enhancement for promotion).

» There may be fear of the unknown which, so long as the approach is working fully, is largely edited out because it is founded on a collective openness and understanding of commercial and operational positions.

» There may be collective and personal resistances based on the comfort and familiarity of the ways in which things are presently done; this is best used as a basis for attitude and behavior development rather than trying to impose sudden transformation. In particular, if new technology or workplace layout is required, then habits and perceptions can be developed alongside proficiency in the new technology or ways of working.

» Business process re-engineering and total quality management-led drives and initiatives which carry universal perceptions of downsizing, right-sizing, resizing and reorganization are all widely believed to mean job losses and lay-offs. If external consultants are being used in pursuit of one of these programs, their brief will include and integrate staff development wherever possible. Lay-offs are considered only as a last resort.

Above all, there is the need to preserve technical, occupational and professional well-being. If radical transformation is the eventual aim, then those in work require what they do now to be substituted with something that is known and understood to be equally valuable to themselves, to the organization, and to individual and collective long-term prosperity.

CONCLUSIONS

Learning organizations address many of the key and current issues facing everyone. They do this by taking a strategic approach to ensure that both behavior and performance are continuously developed. The outcome must be the following.

1 There should be the creation and development of intrinsically worthwhile, productive and valuable jobs acceptable to those who come to work in the particular organization. These must be supported by

the knowledge and understanding that they lead to opportunities for development, enhancement and advancement, and that each of these will be made available on a regular basis. It is also essential that pay, terms and conditions of employment, and other rewards, meet expectations and are commensurate with the levels of technological, occupational and professional capability and commitment required.

2 There must be the creation of a high-quality working environment. This requires attention to technical equipment and furnishings; and also to the establishment and development of the human aspects of the environment. This is supported and enhanced by highly expert open management styles; and these are required whatever the organization structure or culture may be.

3 There should be a strong ethical dimension that reinforces collective and individual general comfort, making the workplace something in which individuals have confidence and pride, as well as being a place of achievement.

4 There must be a clearly understood leadership style with which all can identify and be comfortable. Organizations that have charismatic public figures at the top (e.g. Richard Branson, Jack Welch, Lee Iaccocca) find this more straightforward. Organizations that are led on more traditional lines by lesser known figures must still provide this leadership focus and identity. Those in these positions generate their own internally understood loyalty and identity by ensuring that they regularly visit and are in touch with all parts of their domain.

KEY LEARNING POINTS

The following are all important:

» top management support and focus;
» adequate resources;
» an enlightened approach to success and failure;
» the need to institutionalize all instruments – appraisal, needs analyses, activities, mentoring, monitoring, review and evaluation;

- management development – including willingness and application, as well as capability;
- a strategic approach to development positioned as a crucial instrument in the management of change;
- reinforcement of the need for high-level absolute standards of ethics, morality, integrity and openness;
- the participative nature of decision-making; and
- institutionalizing everything in the long term to give strategic focus and integration.

07

Success Stories in Practice

» The chapter looks at the following case studies:
  - P&O European Ferries Plc
  - Patagonia Inc.
  - Sanyo Inc.
  - Semco Inc.

Each of the examples in this chapter indicates the critical nature of the contribution of individual and collective learning and development to long-term enduring operational success and organizational transformation. Each indicates a different strategic management perspective; however, the end result is the same – the development of an excellent organization in an extremely competitive sector, and in the face of overwhelming operational and environmental difficulties. The examples are:

» P&O European Ferries Plc, the major shipping line responsible for the carriage of passengers and freight between the UK and mainland Europe, and the largest alternative to the Channel Tunnel;
» Patagonia Inc., the high-quality, top brand operator in the US outdoor clothing and equipment sector;
» Sanyo Inc., the Japanese electrical goods manufacturer, now located in many other parts of the world; and
» Semco Inc., the Brazilian white goods, hydraulic pump, and engineering company, often held up as a model of all organization practice.

P&O EUROPEAN FERRIES PLC

P&O took over Townsend–Thoresen, a car ferry operator that plied between Dover, France and Belgium, at the beginning of 1987. It immediately faced problems – the Zeebrugge disaster of 1987, and the seamen's strike of 1988. P&O had therefore to reconstitute and relaunch the ferry services from the port of Dover to France and Belgium virtually from scratch. This was devised, determined and conducted as follows.

The image

The company changed the color scheme of the ships, replacing the distinctive orange, white and green scheme of the previous owners with its own dark blue and white. The distinctive P&O flag was adopted as the logo and focus of attention and was painted on the funnels of all ships. The ships were all renamed – first as *The Pride of Dover*, *The Pride of Calais*, and so on; subsequently, "The Pride of" was dropped so that now the ships are named simply after English and French towns and regions. The freight ships that they operate give an alternative message – the names used on these are all prefixed with the word "European."

The ships and facilities

The ships were specifically designed for operation on this route and to be maneuverable in the confined spaces within the ports of Dover and Calais. In appearance they are also very distinctive and the organization has made a feature of this in its marketing and promotional activities.

The facilities have been emphasized as being suitable to a great range of tastes and requirements. A club or business class is now on offer, having regard to the coming on stream of the Channel Tunnel with its express through passenger trains aimed at business travelers which provides exclusive facilities for this niche. A range of restaurants – waiter service, cafeteria, coffee and burger bars – are available. Exclusive facilities are provided for lorry and coach drivers. The whole impression generated is that of a combination of high quality and excellence of facilities whichever particular niche the member of the travelling public happens to fall into.

Other offerings on board ship include a cinema, computer and video games, extensive onboard shopping and children's play areas.

The service

In terms of *volume*, the company operates up to 100 return crossings per day. This may rise and will depend upon continued increases in traffic volumes between Britain and mainland Europe, and the company's stated desire to operate a shuttle service whereby a ship would leave each port either when it was full, or at the end of every stated period of time, whichever came sooner. The company currently has 16 ships on the route.

In terms of *capacity*, the company's ships are each designed with this particular route in mind. They are able to accommodate up to 2500 passengers per crossing in a variety of combinations – tourist, business, coach and package parties, lorries and heavy haulage, and other commercial travelers. It should be noted that during the depth of the UK recession of 1992, total traffic volume carried between Dover and the mainland nevertheless increased by 11%.

All *staff* complete an extensive induction and orientation program and periods of job training. The emphasis is on the satisfaction of customers and the quality of service required and expected in order to achieve this. Attitudes, behavior, standards of dress and appearance are clearly defined. Smart, yet functional, uniforms are worn by staff, giving both identity and confidence.

Staff relations were reformed in the period following the seamen's strike of 1988 and 1989. The trade union (RMT) was de-recognized by the company; work and shift patterns were altered; the numbers of crew members per ship were reduced; and a much greater flexibility both of rostering, and occupation, was determined. The organization stated that its purpose in doing this was the necessity both to compete with the Channel Tunnel traffic, and to improve the efficiency and effectiveness of the services as they developed and extended in the period following the integration of the single European market.

In terms of *acquisitions*, in 1997 P&O took over the short sea crossing operations of Stena, the Scandinavian multinational, in order to provide a viable alternative to the operations of Eurotunnel, the Channel Tunnel shuttle operator, which carries about half of the total cross-Channel traffic. The company has been able to use this position of being second largest operator to acquire further large and purpose-built ships. The third operator, Sea France, which carries about 7% of the total traffic, has also been able to develop a niche.

In terms of *repositioning*, the company has had to adjust its on-board shopping and merchandizing operations in the wake of the abolition of duty free allowances between member states of the European Union in 1998. The result of this has been to enable travelers to make purchases at French prices, which has partly offset the losses sustained following the abolition of duty free. This remains attractive, especially to British day trip travelers during the autumn, winter and spring.

The strategic purpose behind all this is complex. P&O, first of all, desires to be the major ferry operator in the single European market. It needs to be able to compete with the Eurotunnel as the potential of its operations is realized in the early part of the twenty-first century. It desires also to set standards of service, reliability, confidence and quality that underline its strategy.

The *process* in which the company engaged in transforming the nature, quality and style of its services between Dover, France and Belgium took the best part of three years to achieve. What is in place now is a distinctive, profitable and high-quality service, equipped to compete with the Channel Tunnel and versatile enough to take advantage of any new market opportunities that may be afforded to it on its routes – both in operational terms, and also accommodating any increase in volumes of traffic generated by the continued development of the European market.

KEY INSIGHTS

» The importance of strategic and competitive focus.
» The importance of attending to all aspects, and integrating learning and development activities with everything else that has been undertaken, in order to secure a competitive position.
» The primary importance of staff training, supported with distinctive standards of behavior and performance.
» The importance of ensuring that standards remain high during periods of rapid growth by organizations.
» Learning from past histories – creating the conditions in which past disasters and mishaps cannot possibly recur; and keeping the potential for future disasters and mishaps to an absolute minimum.
» Concentrating all activities, including learning and development, on providing and maintaining a high-quality customer service environment; ensuring that staff are both capable and willing to carry this out.

PATAGONIA INC.

The following is reproduced from N. Compton, "Yvon Chouinard, Man of Patagonia," *Orange Magazine*, summer 2000.

Yvon Chouinard: the man from Patagonia

Take a young person and ask them to name the man behind their favorite fashion label. Many will offer Ralph Lauren, Calvin Klein or

Tommy Hilfiger. But an increasing number of young people will tell you about a balding, weather-beaten 61-year old French-Canadian called Yvon Chouinard.

Now ask a class of ambitious business degree types to nominate a corporate chief executive they admire. Richard Branson, Michael O'Leary and Bill Gates are all obvious choices. But some will also opt for Chouinard. And who was it that inspired an ever-increasing number of young city dwellers to head for the hills in pursuit of the wilderness experience? Again, Chouinard's your man. Ask an environmental activist who helps fund their activities ... well, you get the picture.

Yvon Chouinard is little known in Britain, but in the United States he is an icon. As the founder and head of Patagonia, the brand that ignited the craze for technical outdoor clothing – clothes that are all about functional simplicity – he can claim to be one of the most influential fashion forces of recent years.

But his appeal goes far beyond that of an expert marketeer of fancy pants. Chouinard is perhaps unwittingly the point of convergence for any number of lifestyle trends – a reluctant guru of fashion, business and lifestyle. And ironically the more successful he becomes, the more he tortures himself over what he has created. He may be a hero but he is a complex and unwilling one.

Chouinard was born in 1938 and lived in Maine until he was seven when his parents moved to Burbank, California. Speaking only French-Canadian, the young Chouinard became something of a loner, spending much of his time surfing. An interest in falconry led him to climbing which became his major passion. By the early 60s he was roughing it at Yosemite National Park's legendary Camp Four – to this day, the place that any rock climber dreams of pitching his tent. Chouinard pioneered a number of routes up Yosemite's celebrated peak El Capitan and the valley's other massive rock faces. In doing so, he became a hero of the emerging beatnik climbing scene – reading Jack Kerouac, listening to jazz and delving into Zen Buddhism. Along the way, he supported himself as a blacksmith, producing climbing hardware on a portable forge. An ice axe he designed in 1968 became a permanent exhibit at New York's museum of modern art.

Yet Chouinard was already concerned about the effect of his sport on the environment. Aged 19, he had revolutionized climbing by creating pitons that could be removed from the rock rather than just left to rust. Throughout the 70s and 80s the Patagonia label grew and grew. It became the leading name in outdoor clothing and started to find its way into urban fashion. In 1986, he started to contribute 1% of sales or 10% of pre-tax profits, whichever was the larger, to a wide range of environmental groups, many of them small, local projects. And still Patagonia kept growing. By 1991, sales had reached $100 million.

Then recession hit hard. Chouinard had to lay off 120 of his 620 staff, many of them friends. This setback caused him to have a radical rethink. He began to remodel the company. He began to formulate an idea of sustainable development – natural organic growth. He still limits the Patagonia range and encourages customers only to buy what they absolutely need.

After an environmental audit of the company's production, Chouinard started making fleeces out of recycled plastic bottles. In 1996, he decided to use only organic cotton in Patagonia clothes even though this added 25% to the production costs. Sales dropped 20% but he held steady, even loaning money to organic growers to keep them in business. Everything in the worldwide chain of stores was checked for environmental impact. If he is a man with a moral mission, he also has a faith that what he does will be repaid in profits and that the corporation can be a force for good. *"If you want to change government,"* he says, *"change the corporations and government will follow. To change corporations, change the consumers. Perhaps the real good that we do is to use the company as a tool for social change."*

Patagonia's sales now stand at around $200 million. Chouinard it seems can do no wrong, with the Patagonia model being used by any number of companies who have realized that brand honesty and environmentally responsible production can translate into long-term security and profitability. *"If you focus on the goal and not the process,"* says Chouinard, *"you inevitably compromise. But for me, profit is what happens when you do everything else right. A good cast will always catch a fish."*

This is not enough for Chouinard of course. He is still tormented by the company's success. Patagonia now reaches an audience far beyond the active outdoors types. The Patagonia zip-up jacket is part of a uniform for many young Brits and much of the range has been widely copied. Yet he has a strangely ambivalent attitude to those who use his products for the purpose for which they were intended.

> "Part of the process of life is to question how you live it," he explains. "Nobody takes the time to do things right. With mountain climbing, people are only interested in reaching the top of the peak so that they can tell others that they did it."

However, there is a discrepancy here. The Patagonia catalogue is a glorious call to the wild. Can he really blame stressed out city dwellers for trying to get a bit of fresh air, especially if he allows them to look good and keep warm doing it? Chouinard proposes that the great American wildernesses should be the preserve of a dedicated few, yet his company encourages an exodus of the many. If the surf is crowded and the rock face cluttered, then Patagonia has had a big hand in making it so.

So the question arises: if Chouinard believes that we are consuming ourselves to destruction then why does he dedicate his life to making thermal underpants? It's a matter of compromise and Chouinard acknowledges his own weaknesses.

> "We are an incredibly damaging species and we are pulling all these other beautiful species down with us. Maybe we ought just to get out of here. You do what you can. Then, even if you are burning petrol to get there, you just have to say 'forget it, let's go surfing.'"

Chouinard's contradictions reflect those of our age. We want to heal the planet while stocking up with as many consumer goods as our credit cards will allow. We want to be outdoors but only if we get there in an air-conditioned, four wheel drive and stay in rose covered cottages with modern central heating. Chouinard is a contradictory hero for contradictory times but he is still a hero.

KEY INSIGHTS

» The distinctive nature of organizational leadership in learning and developing organizations.

- » The generation of high and enduring levels of staff commitment.
- » The distinctive relationship between known and perceived high product quality; market and customer reputation; general feelings of confidence; and staff and management capability.
- » The distinctive ethical position – and this includes acknowledging any particular quirks and anomalies that may be apparent.
- » The ability to conduct everything in support of the brand, and product and service confidence – absolute commitment to product and service quality, and to customer and client satisfaction and delight.
- » Recognizing potential for further development.
- » Understanding that a high level of reputation can easily be lost; and establishing forms of organization and management that minimize the chances of this occurring.
- » Establishing high and distinctive leadership qualities and identity.
- » The distinctive moral and ethical stance – the concern for the environment and active steps to contribute to its management and refurbishment.

SANYO INC.

Sanyo Inc. manufactures industrial and consumer white goods and other electrical products for sale and distribution around the world. Out of many Japanese manufacturing companies, the company has adopted a distinctive standpoint of: "high-quality, high-value work in return for high levels of pay and job security."

Formal statement of position

As it has established factories across the world and away from Japan, the company has devised and implemented distinctive standards of attitude, behavior, conformity and performance as it seeks to ensure its long-term security and high reputation of its products.

For the management of its overseas activities, Sanyo Inc. devised a 23-page staff handbook that clearly established the standards, attitudes and values required. It outlined the specific responsibilities and obligations placed on everyone involved in the pursuit of long-term business excellence and performance. The following are excerpts that underpin and reinforce the priority given to individual and collective development and enhancement. The extracts are used with permission of Sanyo Industries (UK) Ltd, Oulton Works, School Road, Lowestoft, Suffolk NR33 9NA, UK (Sanyo (UK) Ltd, 1982).

The Sanyo Industries (UK) Ltd staff handbook

The Company and the Union have agreed to enter this Agreement for the purpose of recognizing various mutual and other objectives which is in the interests of both parties and of the employees of the Company to achieve and accordingly the Company and the Union have agreed the following matters.

1

1.1 The independence of the practices and procedures laid down in the respect of the factory premises at Oulton Works, School Road, Lowestoft ('the Establishment') from time to time.

1.2 The non-federated status of the Establishment established by this Agreement.

1.3 Each of the terms and provisions of this Agreement is dependent upon the observance of all the other terms and provisions, individual provisions cannot be acted upon without consideration of all other relevant provisions in the Agreement.

1.4 For the duration of this Agreement the Union shall have sole recognition and bargaining rights for all employees covered by this Agreement.

2 In order to achieve the above objectives it is agreed that:

2.1 All aspects of the Establishment and its operations will be so organized as to achieve the highest possible level of efficiency performance and job satisfaction so that the Company shall:

a) be competitive and thus remain in business

b) provide continuity and security of employment for an effective work force

c) establish and maintain good working conditions

d) establish and maintain good employee relations and communications by supporting the agreed consultative negotiating grievance and disciplinary procedures set out in this Agreement

2.2 Both parties accept an obligation to ensure that the Establishment will operate with effective working methods with the best utilization of manpower and without the introduction of wasteful and restrictive working practices and this objective will be achieved by:

a) the selection, training, retraining and supplementary training of employees, wherever necessary, to enable such employees to carry out any job

b) the maximum co-operation with and support from all employees for measures and techniques used in any area to improve organization and individual efficiency and to provide objective information with which to control and appraise the performance of individual employees and the Establishment

c) the maximum co-operation and support from all employees in achieving a completely flexible well motivated work force capable of transferring on a temporary or permanent basis into work of any nature that is within the capability of such employee having due regard to the provision of adequate training and safety arrangements.

2.3 Both parties recognize that the well-being of the employees is dependent upon the Company's success and that the high standards of product quality and reliability are essential if the products produced at the Establishment are to become and remain competitive, and that therefore the maximum co-operation and support must be given to measures designed to achieve maintain and improve quality and reliability standards.

3 The following matters have been agreed in connection with the Union:

3.1 Employees will not be required to become union members but the Company will encourage all employees covered by this Agreement to become a member of the Union and participate in Union affairs and in this connection the Company will provide a check off arrangement for the deduction of union subscriptions.

4 It is agreed by the Company and the Union that all matters of difference should wherever possible be resolved at the source of

such difference as speedily as practicable and it is the intention of the parties that all such matters will be dealt with in accordance with the agreed procedure; and in this connection:

5 The Company and the Union will establish a Joint Negotiation Council ('JNC') for the purpose of providing a forum through which discussions regarding improvements to employment conditions and other major matters can be discussed; and in this connection:

    5.1 The JNC will consist of representatives from the Company including the Head of Personnel and Senior Company Representatives and on behalf of the Union the Senior Representative from Production/Warehousing one constituency representative from Administration.

    5.2 Discussions regarding substantive improvements to employment conditions will normally be held on an annual basis during December in each year and such discussions will not include changes arising as a result of promotions transfers or changes to job content which can be implemented at any time as agreed.

6 In addition to the JNC the Company will establish a Joint Consultative Council ('JCC') and the following provisions shall apply thereto:

    6.1 The membership of the JCC shall consist of the Head of Personnel (as Chairman) and appropriate members of the Company's Senior Executives and the Senior Representative together with one constituency representative from each of Production, Engineering and Administration and a further constituency representative on a rotating basis as a co-opted member, and in addition the Managing Director of the Company shall act as President of the JCC and shall attend meetings from time to time.

    6.2 The JCC shall meet on a monthly basis for the purposes of discussing issues of a mutual nature and one week prior to each JCC meeting the Personnel Officer will publish an Agenda agreed with the Senior Representative who will be responsible for submitting items for discussion on behalf of the Union in time for such items to be included on the Agenda.

    6.3 Items to be included for discussion at JCC meetings will include:

        a) manufacturing performance

        b) operating efficiency

        c) manufacturing planning

d) employment levels

e) market information

f) establishment environment

g) employment legislation

h) union policies and procedure

i) level of union membership.

6.4 Following each meeting of the JCC the Head of Personnel will be responsible for communicating to all employees the nature and content of the discussions, and in this connection the Company and the Union recognize the need to conduct meetings of the JCC in constructive manner for the benefit of the Company and all its employees.

7 In the event that the Company and the Union shall be unable ultimately to resolve between themselves any discussions or disputes they may jointly agree to appoint an arbitrator; and in this connection:

7.1 The Arbitrator will consider evidence presented to him by the Company and the Union and any factors that he believes to be appropriate.

7.2 The Arbitrator will decide in favor of one party.

7.3 The decision of the Arbitrator will be final and binding and will represent the final solution to the issue.

8 DISCIPLINARY MEASURES

It is in the interest of the Company and its employees to maintain fair and consistent standards of conduct and performance. This procedure is designed to clarify the rights and responsibilities of the Company, the Union and employees with regard to disciplinary measures.

Principles

The following principles will be followed in applying this procedure:

8.1 In the normal course of their duties, the Company will make employees aware of any shortcomings in performance or conduct. This counseling stage is separate from the disciplinary procedure as such.

8.2 When the disciplinary procedure is invoked, the intention is to make the employee aware that the Company is concerned with their conduct or performance and to assist the person to improve to a satisfactory level.

8.3 When any disciplinary case is being considered, the Company will be responsible for fully investigating the facts and circumstances of the case.

8.4 The procedure will operate as quickly as possible, consistent with the thorough investigation of the case.

8.5 The employee will always be informed of any disciplinary action to be taken and the reasons for it, indicating the specific areas for improvement.

8.6 Normally the formal procedure will commence with the issuing of the first formal warning; however, the disciplinary procedure may be invoked at any stage depending on the seriousness of the case.

8.7 Each formal warning will apply for 12 months. Should the employee improve their conduct or performance to an acceptable level and maintain the improvement for the duration of the warning, this will result in the deletion of the warning from their record.

Dated this 10th day of June 1982

KEY INSIGHTS

» The importance and value of formalized statements and procedures in support of developing high-quality workplace and occupational activities.

» The importance of training, retraining and supplementary training of employees wherever necessary.

» The securing of maximum cooperation from employees and their recognized trade union as a condition of employment.

» Distinctive joint consultative counsel responsibilities for organization and employee development.

» Procedures, institutions and mechanisms for speedy resolution of disagreements, disputes, grievances, disciplinary matters and issues concerning poor performance.

» Commitment to ensure that pay and conditions are improved by agreement and consultation whenever these become required.
» The joint nature of the approach – with especial reference to the role of the recognized union, reflecting the company's absolute commitment to openness and transparency of activities.
» The implicit need for managerial expertise and integrity – if problems cannot be resolved as stated, or employees managed as stated, then the whole clearly falls.
» The use of unionization and union recognition in the collective development of attitudes, values, standards and expertise.
» The willingness of the company to subject its standards to union scrutiny.
» The acceptance of overall responsibility by the company for individual and collective development.

SEMCO INC.

The following is reproduced from *Maverick* by R. Semler (Century, 1992).

Learning organizations and upwards/360-degree appraisal and management development

"Semco is more than novel programs or procedures. What is important is our open-mindedness, our trust in our employees and distrust of dogma. We are neither socialist nor purely capitalist. We take the best of everything to reorganize work so that collective thinking does not overpower individualistic flights of grandeur; that leadership does not get lost in an endless search for consensus; that people are free to work as they like, when they like; that bosses don't have to be parents and workers don't act like children. At the heart of our bold experiment is a truth so simple it would be silly if it wasn't so rarely recognized – **a company should trust its destiny to its employees**."

Accordingly, the company regularly asks its employees to evaluate its managerial staff. Every six months, a formal questionnaire is anonymously completed by all Semco employees as part of this process. The questions are weighted according to their importance and the results are published. There are 36 questions and a score out of 100 is given.

A score of 80 out of 100 is average for Semco managers. Scores of 70 and below are causes for concern; and the further below a score of 70 that is achieved, the greater the corporate concern. The view is taken that, so long as employees are frank and honest, managers understand what is important to the company, and their employees, as well as themselves, therefore long-term, sustainable and positive management styles, and therefore OD, is assured.

The coverage of the questionnaire is as follows.

1 When an employee makes a small mistake, the manager is:
   a) irritated and unwilling to discuss the mistake;
   b) irritated but willing to discuss it;
   c) realizes the mistake and discusses it in a constructive manner;
   d) ignores the mistake and only pays attention to more important matters.
2 The manager reacts to criticism:
   a) poorly, ignoring it;
   b) poorly, rejecting it;
   c) reasonably well;
   d) well, accepting it.
3 The manager is:
   a) constantly tense;
   b) usually tense, but relaxed on occasions;
   c) usually relaxed, but tense on occasions;
   d) constantly relaxed.
4 When an employee makes a small mistake, the manager is:
   a) irritated and unwilling to discuss the mistake;
   b) irritated but willing to discuss it;
   c) realizes the mistake and discusses it in a constructive manner;
   d) ignores the mistake and only pays attention to more important matters.

5 The manager reacts to criticism:
   a) poorly, ignoring it;
   b) poorly, rejecting it;
   c) reasonably well;
   d) well, accepting it.

6 The manager is:
   a) constantly tense;
   b) usually tense, but relaxed on occasions;
   c) usually relaxed, but tense on occasions;
   d) constantly relaxed.

7 The manager is:
   a) insecure;
   b) more often insecure than secure;
   c) more often secure than insecure;
   d) secure.

8 As far as professional and personal relationships are concerned, the manager is:
   a) incapable of separating them;
   b) frequently incapable of separating them;
   c) usually capable of separating them;
   d) capable of separating them.

9 When the manager's department achieves a high level of productivity he/she usually:
   a) takes credit for other's success;
   b) gives credit to those who did the work;
   c) gives credit to the team as a whole.

10 The manager is seen as:
   a) always unfair;
   b) more often unfair than fair;
   c) more often fair than unfair;
   d) always fair.

11 The manager conveys to his/her team feelings of:
   a) fear and insecurity;
   b) indifference;
   c) security and tranquility.

12 The manager transmits to his/her team a sense of:
    a) coldness and unwillingness to talk;
    b) distance, but willingness to talk;
    c) friendliness, but indifference to other's problems;
    d) friendliness and concern with other's problems.
13 When dealing with people in inferior positions, the manager usually:
    a) has an attitude of superiority;
    b) ignores them;
    c) treats them politely but with an air of superiority;
    d) respects them.
14 Managers treat their subordinates:
    a) much worse than they treat their superiors;
    b) a little worse than they treat their superiors;
    c) treats both the same.
15 The manager:
    a) constantly reminds everyone he/she is the boss;
    b) occasionally reminds everyone he/she is the boss;
    c) rarely makes a point of being the boss.
16 The manager is:
    a) a weak leader, unable to motivate the team;
    b) a weak leader, but able to motivate the team;
    c) a strong leader, but unable to motivate the team;
    d) a strong leader and able to motivate the team.
17 When the team has a specific goal, the manager:
    a) demands results, but doesn't participate in the effort to achieve them;
    b) demands results and participates superficially;
    c) participates in the efforts when necessary to meet the goal.
18 The manager:
    a) is openly held in disrespect by the team;
    b) is held in disrespect by the team, but not publicly;
    c) generates neither respect nor disrespect;
    d) is respected by the team.
19 The manager:
    a) gives obvious preferential treatment to some people because of their color, religion or origin;

b) denies being biased but doesn't give equal opportunity to everyone;

c) isn't biased and gives equal opportunity to everyone.

20 The manager:

a) gives obvious preference to people of a certain gender;

b) denies being biased but doesn't give equal opportunity to everyone;

c) isn't biased and gives equal opportunity to everyone.

21 Where promotions and prizes are concerned, the manager:

a) gives them out to those he/she likes;

b) sometimes gives them to those who deserve them, and sometimes gives them to followers;

c) almost always is just and impartial.

22 During a crisis, the manager:

a) disrupts the group's unity;

b) doesn't affect the group's unity;

c) helps the group stick together.

23 Which is more important to the manager:

a) work to be performed perfectly;

b) work to be performed quickly;

c) either speed or perfection depending on the situation.

24 The manager is:

a) excessively involved in all situations;

b) not involved enough in all situations;

c) adequately involved in all situations.

25 The manager's knowledge of his/her area is:

a) insufficient;

b) sufficient;

c) profound.

26 If the manager were to replace you temporarily, his/her performance would be:

a) unsatisfactory;

b) regular;

c) good;

d) better than yours.

27 In choosing between the urgent and the important, the manager:
   a) doesn't know the difference;
   b) usually tends towards the urgent;
   c) distinguishes well between the two.

28 The manager:
   a) wastes too much time on urgent problems;
   b) gives equal time to urgent and important matters;
   c) gives more time to important matters.

29 The manager is:
   a) not very creative and resists new ideas;
   b) too creative and change-oriented, disturbing the atmosphere;
   c) is adequately creative and change-oriented.

30 As far as creating an environment where people are free to be creative or suggest changes, the manager:
   a) blocks innovative and creative ideas;
   b) doesn't block them, but also doesn't create them;
   c) promotes creative or innovative ideas.

31 As far as the team is concerned, the manager:
   a) usually chooses the wrong people;
   b) sometimes chooses well and sometimes chooses poorly;
   c) usually chooses the right people.

32 The people who work around the manager:
   a) rarely feel motivated to work;
   b) sometimes feel motivated to work;
   c) usually feel motivated to work.

33 The manager's use of financial resources is:
   a) poor;
   b) average;
   c) good;
   d) excellent.

34 The manager's use of his/her own time is:
   a) bad;
   b) average;
   c) good;
   d) excellent.

35 The value the manager gives to training and related matters is:
   a) too small;
   b) sufficient;
   c) too great.

36 The manager performs tasks:
   a) almost always poorly;
   b) sometimes poorly and sometimes well;
   c) almost always well.

37 Regarding opinions that differ from theirs, the manager:
   a) never accepts them;
   b) usually doesn't accept them;
   c) sometimes accepts them;
   d) almost always accepts them.

38 People find the manager:
   a) untrustworthy;
   b) occasionally untrustworthy;
   c) very trustworthy.

39 The manager represents the company:
   a) poorly raising concern about it;
   b) neither poorly nor well;
   c) well, leading people to trust it.

This questionnaire is filled in by all staff as a prelude to frank, open and honest discussions about managers and their performance. The purpose is to ensure that managers understand what is expected of them by both the company and their staff. The questions are frank and direct; however, the discussions that arise as the result concentrate solely on improving business, organizational and managerial performance. Many of the questions are about the conditions in which work is carried out, and the nature of relationships engendered between managers and subordinates.

Managers understand that they have to go through this process. It is in the interests of everyone, therefore, that they take responsibility for developing their management style from the basis of enthusiasm, openness, integrity and commitment; if they do not, this will show up in this form of ranking and appraisal activity.

KEY INSIGHTS

» The importance of openness, honesty, integrity and trust.
» The importance of generating positive and committed attitudes.

- The importance and value of management development.
- The importance of creating collective, shared and positive attitudes, values and culture as a precursor to effective discussions of this kind.
- The contribution that this form of rigorous appraisal makes to long-term and effective business and managerial performance.
- The focus of this form of appraisal on the development of collective attitudes, values and beliefs; high standards of behavior and confidence; and effective long-term operational activities.
- The contribution of this form of appraisal to long-term, enduring and effective business performance.

08

Key Concepts and Thinkers

» Glossary of terms.
» Related concepts and thinkers.

A GLOSSARY FOR THE LEARNING ORGANIZATION

Attitudes – The mental, moral and ethical dispositions adopted by individuals to others and their situation and environment.

Computer-based training (CBT) – Organizational, collective and individual development efforts undertaken with a view to either develop proficiency in technological usage and awareness, or to use computer technology as the medium for delivering training and development activities.

Continuous professional or occupational development (CPD or COD) – Formal or institutional requirements for those in certain occupations and professions to keep their skills, knowledge and expertise up to date.

Coaching – The development of specific expertise by one who is proficient to another who is not.

Core training and development programs – The body of skills, knowledge, attitudes and behavior required by organizations of their staff, which is commenced at induction and reinforced with initial and continuing job and workplace training and development.

Counseling – A collective or individual advisory service, or advice on specific initiatives or activities.

Employee development – Activities structured to enhance and improve all aspects of staff and employee performance.

Employability – The outcome of structured training and development activities, enhancing the value of both individuals and groups to their organization, and to the labor market at large.

Factory improvement groups – Groups constituted in factory and production-oriented working situations to attend to improvements in the quality of working life, product delivery and productivity, and improvements in processes and procedures.

Group development – Activities that have the primary purpose of improving and enhancing the work output and professional and personal cohesion of groups of people.

Management development – Structured initiatives and activities that have the purpose of enhancing management, supervisory and leadership style, content and effectiveness.

Mentor – One who adopts the role of advisor, guide, energizer, sounding board and cheerleader to another as they pursue project and other development work.

Occupational development – A series of activities, the end result of which is to make individuals more proficient at their specific occupation, and which begin to identify potential for both occupational and individual enhancement and enlargement.

Off-the-job training – Training and development activities which are provided away from the place of work (e.g. taught courses, university and college courses, short courses, outward bound, and practical activities).

On-the-job training – Events designed to improve performance that take place at the individual's place of work (e.g. project work, technological proficiency development, simulators and simulations.

Organization development (OD) – The UK definition of the "learning organization."

Profession – Anything that has a distinctive status, body of expertise, self-examination and self-regulation; the classical professions medicine, the law, the military and the priesthood.

Projects – A specific activity with its own remit and terms of reference, timescale, desired outputs, and conclusions; many projects carry recommendations for courses of action and lead on to other things.

Quality circles – Groups of staff drawn together from within organizations to address particular issues concerning quality of working life, quality of product and service delivery.

Quality improvement groups – Groups of staff drawn together from within organizations to address particular issues and problems surrounding product and service quality.

Quality of working life – The phrase used to summarize the individual and collective experience at the place of work, and which reflects the nature of technology, equipment, furnishings, comfort and management style present.

Strategy – An orderly, prescribed and accepted approach to business and organizational direction, priority and performance.

Secondment – The removal of individuals and/or groups from their normal place of work for a particular purpose; secondments are offered to individuals, for example, in order to enhance their general familiarity and understanding of the ways in which organizations work, or as part of pursuing a particular project or initiative; groups may also be seconded for particular purposes, e.g. to brainstorm a particular problem, or to address and resolve an issue very quickly.

Vocational education and training (VET) – The terms used (in the UK especially) to describe the particular emphasis placed by some organizations, institutions and occupations on technical and occupational employee and collective development; this, above all, refers to proficiency in practical subjects and activities.

Work improvement groups (WIGs) – Groups constituted from within organizations to address particular aspects of production, service delivery, and the processes, practices and procedures that support these.

KEY CONCEPTS AND THINKERS

The relationship between achievement and motivation

The nature of the relationship between capability and willingness to work was defined as the result of studies carried out by McClelland in the 1950s and 1960s. McClelland identified the relationship between personal characteristics, social and general background, and achievement.

Persons with high needs for achievement exhibited the following characteristics.

» Task rather than relationship orientation.
» A preference for tasks over which they had sole or overriding control and responsibility.
» The need to identify closely, and be identified closely, with the successful outcomes of their action.
» Task balance. This had to be difficult enough, on the one hand, to be challenging and rewarding; to be capable of demonstrating expertise and good results; and to be capable of gaining status and recognition from others. On the other hand, it needed to be

moderate enough to be capable of demonstrable successful achievement.

» Risk balance. The individual seeks to avoid, as far as possible, the likelihood and consequences of failure.
» The need for feedback on the results achieved to reinforce the knowledge of success, and to ensure that successes were validated and publicized.
» The need for progress, variety and opportunity.

The need for achievement is based on a combination of:

» intrinsic motivation – the drives from within the individual; and
» extrinsic motivation – the drives, pressures and expectations exerted by the organization, peers and society.

As well as identifying the relationship between capability and willingness, McClelland also identified a key factor in the development of collective and individual skills, knowledge, attitudes, behavior and expertise. Those with high needs for achievement, and high professional and occupational qualifications, need a combination of variety and challenge; and at the same time, they need extensive organizational support if they are to be fully effective. Those working in organizations where these characteristics and occupations are present therefore need to be aware of the need to provide institutional support, as well as individual and group opportunities.

McClelland also identified a problem in relation to the appointment of high achievers to responsible managerial and supervisory positions. Because the high achiever tended to be task, rather than relationship, driven, many neither possessed nor regarded as important the human relations characteristics necessary to get things done through people, or to pay sufficient attention to the wider elements of the human side of enterprise.

Highlights

Books:

» McClelland, D.C. (1960, 1988) *Human Motivation*. Cambridge University Press, Cambridge.

Self-actualization

Self-actualization is a key concept in the understanding of human motivation and a key drive in individual and collective development. First used by Maslow and Schein, self-actualization refers to people's ability and drive to realize their full potential to progress as far as possible and to be fulfilled; and to have this recognized and valued by others. Self-actualization addresses the need for challenge, responsibility, variety, pride and development in work and achievement, as well as technological and professional expertise. The ability to fulfill potential is affected by society, cultural background, norms and values.

Two views of self-actualization are taken. The first is that self-actualization is available only to the very few. It is limited by the inability to develop sufficient qualities and capabilities for this to take place. This is due to the limitations of the social background of many people and, above all, education, training and other means by which skills, knowledge and expertise are developed.

The alternative view is that self-actualization is achievable by almost everyone in their own particular circumstances. Whatever the limitations placed by society, education and occupation, individuals nevertheless exhibit a range of capabilities and qualities that have the potential of being harnessed and developed in the pursuit of highly rewarding lives in their own terms. Self-actualization is therefore an individual and not an absolute process.

The latter view is current. It is reinforced by the experiences of organizations that have adopted these approaches; and especially of the potential for self-actualization in production environments as espoused by Japanese manufacturing companies. It is of particular value in understanding that everyone has needs for respect, value and esteem. Whatever the nature, level or content of work carried out, people will tend to seek variety and enhancement if this is at all possible; if it is not possible at present, people will tend to seek it elsewhere, whether by changing jobs or else in their lives outside work.

This view tends to militate against traditional and classical organization features of task specialization, administrative hierarchies, and division of work, which expect individuals to restrict their capabilities, work as directed, and operate machinery and systems, rather than develop and use their capabilities and talents to the full.

Highlights

Books:

» Maslow, A. (1960, 1987) *Motivation and Personality*. Harper & Row, London.
» Schein, E. (1974) *Organizational Psychology*. Prentice Hall, Hounslow.

The relationship between motivation, achievement and rewards

One view of the effectiveness of using learning and development as a performance management strategy lies in drawing together the relationship between motivation, achievement and rewards. Drives to particular goals are enhanced by the capability to achieve them and the rewards that are to accrue as the result. These rewards are a combination of the following factors.

» *Economic*: monetary pay for carrying out work, for special achievement, for responsibility and accountability. This is expected to continue and improve in line with the relationship between the organization and the individual, both in terms of current and future occupations, and also loyalty and commitment. Economic rewards meet the needs and expectations of individuals, and also reflect the value in which they are held by the organization.
» *Job and work satisfaction*: intrinsic rewards attained by individuals in terms of the quality of their work, the range and depth of expertise used and the results achieved.
» *Work content*: the relative contribution to the output of the organization as a whole, and feelings of success and achievement that arise from this. Operating a small part of production processes or administrative systems tends to be limited in its capability to satisfy this part of the requirement for achievement; and tends therefore to reinforce the need for work flexibility, enhancement, enrichment, rotation and enlargement.
» *Job titles*: certain job titles give images of prestige, as well as a description and summary of what the work is. In many circles, this reinforces the wider general feelings of respect, value and esteem in which individuals are held by their peers and social circles.

» *Personal development*: the extent to which individual capabilities are being used or limited in their use; and the extent to which alternative means of achievement and reward may become apparent through the development of both current and new expertise.

» *Status*: the relative mark of value placed on the individual's rank, role, expertise and occupation by those whose views and opinions they value. This invariably includes those of the particular organization, because of the relationship between status and economic reward.

» *Trappings*: these are the outward marks of achievement and success, and many people need to exhibit them in return for recognition. These include benefits such as cars; healthcare; other business technology (e.g. personal computer, laptop); business trips; sabbaticals; course and seminar attendance.

» *Autonomy*: the ability of individuals to establish their own patterns of work; to come and go as they see fit; to work from home; to attend the place of work at weekends or other quiet periods in order to be able to work without interruptions; to make work arrangements based on sole individual judgement without reference to higher authorities; to exhibit absolute professional or technical expertise and judgement.

» *Secretaries, personal assistants and staff officers*: normally integral to the nature of work, they also constitute a trapping in so far as they are an outward representation to the rest of the organization of the perceived value and importance of the particular individual and their work.

» *Accessibility*: in many organizations the inability to get to see someone, either because of their rank or their workload, constitutes a mark of achievement (however perverse this may be in some cases).

Problems and issues surrounding each of these elements do not lie in their validity. Many of these are subjective judgements based on perceptions, expectations and individual requirements for recognition. They do, however, indicate a key part of the relationship between the organization and its staff; and if this is what the staff want, then organizations must be prepared to develop these elements, or to substitute something else of value in their place, or recognize that they will incur staffing problems from time to time.

Highlights

Books:

» Porter, L.W. & Lawler, E.E. (1968, 1998) *Managerial Attitudes and Performance*. Irwin McGraw-Hill, New York.

The implementation of strategy; integrating behavioral and operational drives in the achievement of commitment to purpose

The determination of strategy can be usefully thought of as a combination of four elements:

» examination of the organization's environment for opportunity and risk;
» careful assessment of corporate strengths and weaknesses;
» identification and weighing of personal values built into the character of the organization and its leadership; and
» the establishment of ethical and social responsibility to which it will hold itself.

The assumption that strategy is essentially a value-free appraisal and choice of economic opportunity and evaluation of results – without reference to organization capability, personal values and entrenched cultural loyalties – often led to strategic recommendations by think-tanks and consulting firms that organizations were neither able, nor willing, to carry out. Many planning techniques useful in limited application developed as quick-fix solutions to the need for better performance in competition. Goals often tended to be expressed in terms of high growth rate in sales and profits, mindlessly compounded over future years. Economic objectives were chosen more for their theoretical growth potential than from company capability to attain them. Financial strategies following a modern "theory" divorced from the concept of corporate strategy tend to focus on the acquisition and divestment of assets without reference to impact on human resources, future development and the capacity to manage debt incurred should there be economic adversity.

The catalogue of strategic mismanagement made possible by ignoring the human, social and ethical elements in the pattern of corporate

purpose is universal and overwhelming. Poor performance in competitive markets has exposed overrated techniques and fashionable and
faddish approaches to management. The backlash against strategic
planning that has occurred over the past twenty years is largely justi-
fied and wholly understandable. It has, however, produced its own
distortions. Organizations cannot have purposes without reference to
their staff; and so strategic planning has to take place in the context
that implementation is to be achieved through the capability, expertise, willingness and commitment of those who work in the particular
organization – rather than ignoring them altogether, or assuming that
they will indeed perform when they are told to do so, or when the
particular strategy demands it.

Nor should organization and strategic development be seen in terms
of attractive inanities such as:

» ''moving closer to the customer''
» ''managing by walking around''
» ''fostering continuous innovation.''

The secret lies in the doing. How leadership and top management
should behave is missing from these prescriptions. Explicit strategy is
required to encourage something to happen in the close relationship to
customers, to identify what managers should have in mind when they
walk around, and to suggest constructive direction and completion of
innovations. These are the key contributions to strategic management,
and the implementation of business and organizational priorities and
direction.

Highlights

Books:

» Christensen, C.R. (1987) *Business Policy*. Irwin McGraw-Hill,
New York.

Managing the working environment

The contribution of learning and development to the effective management of the working environment is most effective when it addresses
the following.

» Management style, attitude and approach to staff – this should be based on integrity, honesty and trust whatever the nature, limitations or technology concerned in the work itself.

» The general environment which is to be comfortable, functional and suitable in human terms – again, whatever the occupational constraints and limitations may be. It is important to recognize that where

   – *physical distances*, the actual proximity of staff to each other, are too great or hampered by noise or other operational extremes, and/or

   – *psychological distances* exist based on rank, status, forms of address and differentiation in treatment

then there is in turn the potential for alienation – the loss of identity between organization and its staff.

» Fundamental equality of treatment that transcends status and importance by rank, hierarchy or occupation which ensures that every member of staff is respected, believed in, treated fairly and given opportunity for development and advancement within the organization.

» Effective and professional operational relationships between members of staff that, in turn, promote profitable and successful activities. This includes recognizing the existence of barriers and potential conflicts between departments, divisions and functions, and taking steps to provide effective counters.

» Administrative support and control processes, and reporting relationships must be designed to make life easy for those working at the frontline while, at the same time, providing the necessary management information. This particularly refers to the nature and effectiveness of the roles and functions of corporate headquarters; and the relationships between these and the frontline operations present. The matter is compounded when the organization operates in many different physical locations, as well as different industrial and commercial sectors.

» The work itself and how it is divided up. There is particular reference here to those parts of the work that are looked upon with disfavor but which nevertheless must be carried out adequately and effectively.

» Workplace security, ensuring that people are employed on a continuous basis as far as that is possible. Steps have to be taken to ensure that there is a steady and open flow of development activities in order to enhance both expertise and attitudes, and to engage a positive and forward-looking collective culture.

Highlights

Books:

» Herzberg, F. (1960, 1974, 1994) *Work and the Nature of Man*. Granada, London.

Leadership direction

The following are examples of clear statements by organization leaders indicating a clear set of values by which the organization should – and will – be developed.

"The guiding principle on which Mary Kay cosmetics is based is: do as you would be done by. None of my staff should behave towards customers and clients in any way with which they themselves would be uncomfortable were the positions reversed."

Mary Kay Ash

"We will look at any business proposition, any venture, provided that it satisfies at least four of the following criteria:

» There must be an existing and proven market.
» That market must be capable of development and further improvement and enhancement if a strong quality operator comes into it. Everything that we have gone into has been well established but ill served by existing players.
» The product or service must be ethical. We will not go into tobacco products for example.
» It must reinforce and enhance the Virgin brand and name in positive ways.
» There must also be a sense of cheekiness and of fun.

All our staff are expected to behave in ways that support this."

Richard Branson

"The Body Shop stands for the highest possible ethical and moral standpoint in terms of trading with those who supply it, and satisfying those who come to us as customers. One of the main reasons why I began the Body Shop as a chain of shops was because of the low standards and expectations in the rest of the department store sector."

Anita Roddick

"I was always conscious of the fact that I was making people do something that they did not want to do – i.e. come to work. They would much rather be doing other things. So the first thing that we had to do was to make the place of work somewhere where people actually wanted to be."

Ricardo Semler

Sources

» Ash, M.K. (1990) *On People Management*. Sage, London.
» Branson, R., spoken on *The Money Programme* (BBC, 1998).
» Roddick, A. (1998) *Body and Soul*. Ebury, London.
» Semler, R. (1996) *The Maverick Solution*. BBC, London.

09

Resources for the Learning Organization

» The chapter looks at the contributions of:
- Hofstede
- Drucker
- Heller
- Argyris and Schon
- Senge
- Gratton.
» Further reading.

This chapter contains summaries of the views of acknowledged experts in the field of management. As stated earlier (see Chapters 2 and 3), there is no distinctive or prescribed body of knowledge and expertise in this field. However, each of the works described here emphasizes, from its own distinctive standpoint, the key contribution that individual and collective staff and organization development make to long-term sustainable viability, effectiveness and profitability.

At the end of the chapter there is a list of further reading.

G. HOFSTEDE

» *Cultures and Consequences* (Sage, 1980)

Hofstede's work emphasizes the importance of cultural factors and differences in all areas and aspects of organizational behavior and development. It indicates both the strength and interaction of cultural pressures. It indicates the source and nature of particular values, drives, barriers and blockages; and the behavioral issues and problems that have to be considered. It illustrates the relative strengths of some of the main cultural and social pressures that are brought to bear on all organizations in all situations, and emphasizes the need for the development of collective attitudes, values and standards of behavior as a key element of learning organizations.

Hofstede carried out studies that identified cultural similarities and differences among the 116,000 staff of IBM located in 40 countries. He identified basic dimensions of national culture and the differences in their emphases and importance in various countries. The four dimensions were as set out below.

» *Power-distance* – the extent to which power and influence is distributed across the society; the extent to which this is acceptable to the members of the society; access to sources of power and influence; and the physical and psychological distance that exists between people and the sources of power and influence.
» *Uncertainty-avoidance* – the extent to which people prefer order and certainty, or uncertainty and ambiguity; and the extent to which they feel comfortable or threatened by the presence or absence of each.

» *Individualism-collectivism* - the extent to which individuals are expected, or expect, to take care of themselves; the extent to which a common good is perceived and a tendency and willingness to work towards this.

» *Masculinity-femininity* - the distinction between masculine values (the acquisition of money, wealth, fortune, success, status, ambition and possessions) and the feminine (sensitivity, care, concern, attention to the needs of others, quality of life); and the value, importance, mix and prevalence of each.

Power-distance

The study looked at the extent to which managers and supervisors were encouraged or expected to exercise power and to take it upon themselves to provide order and discipline. For example, in Spain this expectation was very high. Relationships between superior and subordinates were based on low levels of mutual trust, participation and involvement. Employees would accept orders and direction on the understanding that the superior carries full responsibility, authority and accountability. Elsewhere, for example in Australia and Holland, people expected to be consulted and to participate in decision-making. They expected to be kept regularly and fully informed of progress, and had much greater need for general equality and honesty of approach. They would feel free to question superiors about why particular courses of action were necessary, rather than simply accepting that they were.

Uncertainty-avoidance

People with a high propensity for uncertainty-avoidance (those that wished for high degrees of certainty) tended to require much greater volumes of rules, regulations and guidance for all aspects of work. They sought stability and conformity. They were intolerant of dissenters. Uncertainty caused stress, strain, conflicts and disputes. Stress could be avoided by working hard, following the company line and compliance with required ways of behavior. Where uncertainty-avoidance was lower, these forms of stress were less apparent. There was less attention paid to rules; and less emphasis placed on conformity and adherence.

Individualism-collectivism

The concern here was to establish the relative position of individual achievement in terms of that of the organization, as well as in the wider contribution to society and the community. In the UK and USA, overwhelming emphasis was placed on individual performance and achievement. This has implications for membership and development of teams and groups, and the creation of effective collective operations in these locations. It also indicates the extent and likelihood of divergence of purpose between the organization and individuals. Where collectivism was higher, there was a much greater emphasis on harmony, loyalty, support and productive interaction. There was also a much greater priority given to organizational, as distinct from individual, performance.

Masculinity-femininity

This considered the value placed on different achievements. Cultures with high degrees of masculinity set great store by the achievement of material possessions, trappings and rewards. Those with high degrees of femininity saw success in terms of quality of life, general state of the community, individual and collective well-being and the capability to support the whole society and provide security.

P. DRUCKER

» *Management Challenges for the 21st Century* (HarperCollins, 2000)

The approach taken here is to stand much of conventional wisdom in terms of organization and management on its head. Peter Drucker addresses each of the elements of: strategy, change, information, productivity, and the acceptance of responsibility, in terms that require shifts away from structured organizations and towards the harnessing of expertise in the pursuit of long-term and sustainable viability.

The overarching approach concentrates on "the one right way" to organize and manage. However, the "one right way" is to design, develop and create organizations that fit the task, rather than to fit activities into existing organization formats and hierarchies.

The major task of managing is leadership. The view is taken that the manager acts as the equivalent of the conductor of an orchestra. The primary role is therefore to lead, harmonize and integrate all of the diverse activities so that the whole is created by those who actually know what they are doing. This responsibility also includes creating conditions in which this works and is effective, rather than trying to regiment experts into prescribed formalized activities. Drucker takes the view that, because those in professional, technical and other occupations are so highly trained, they clearly are much better able to decide how tasks should actually be carried out than those for whom they work. A fundamental shift of attitude is therefore required of managers in accepting and acknowledging this, and in developing their own expertise to make this effective.

Drucker takes the attitude that "one cannot manage change, one can only be ahead of it." The task of the organization is therefore to lead change and to develop policies that ensure that the future is secured by anticipating and introducing change, and balancing this with continuity. Organizations require collective attitudes of receptiveness to change, and the willingness and ability to change what is already being done as a prerequisite. The key to this is creating and developing policies for innovation based on identifying windows of opportunity. These are identified as:

» the unexpected successes and unexpected failures of both the particular organization and also its competitors;
» incongruities in production and distribution processes, and in customer and client behavior;
» process needs;
» changes in industry, sectoral and market structures; and
» changes in meanings and perceptions.

The relationship between innovation and risk is identified. Any innovation carries with it the possibility of failure, or of leading the organization away from present and comfortable activities. Attitudes that accept and embrace these elements are required.

Innovation must not be confused with novelty. The test of innovations is that they create value; while novelties create only diversion. A distinction must be drawn between whether the organization and those in responsible positions *like* something; and whether customers *want* what is proposed, and whether they are prepared to pay for it. Above all, organizations should never confuse action with effectiveness. The fact that people are busy does not make them effective; the fact that organizations are busy with change policies and processes does not mean that they will be successful in the future.

KEY QUOTE

"We never had time to do anything properly. Consequently, we always had to find time to do it twice."
Suetonius, G., *The Twelve Caesars* (Penguin Classics, 1994; originally written in 120 AD)

The requirement is therefore to develop focus, concentration and direction, as well as positive and willing attitudes.

The development of organizations is based on the access to, and availability of, quality of information, both universally and within the organization. This is referred to as the shift from the technology emphasis, to the information emphasis, in IT. The view is advanced that knowledge worker production, and the application of expertise, is the key to long-term security for organizations and staff. Those with expertise are effectively "capital assets." The costs of labor turnover, rehiring and retraining all add to workforce costs. A fundamental shift is required away from the perception that the management of people at work is based on the premise that "one worker is very much like any other." Because expertise is within, it is totally portable and can be applied anywhere. Management's duty, therefore, is to preserve these particular assets and to develop them. This is required alongside enduring organizational relationships, developing both the skills, qualities and expertise, and also loyalty and identity. The management of experts requires a fundamental understanding of the long-term mutually beneficial relationship that should exist when those with distinctive and required qualities are engaged to produce products and services that customers and clients require.

The final element is the need to manage oneself. This requires acceptance of social and ethical responsibilities, as well as individual commitment to job, occupation, profession or expertise.

The broad view is that all organization managerial, professional and occupational activities depend on social acceptance for economic returns. All activities are conducted ultimately for the good of society and must be acceptable at this level if economic prosperity is to follow.

> "The challenges and issues discussed are already with us in every one of the developed countries and in many of the emerging ones. They can already be identified, discussed, analyzed and prescribed for. Some people are already working on them. But so far, very few organizations do, and very few executives. Those who do work on these challenges today and thus prepare themselves and their institutions for the new challenges will be the leaders and dominate tomorrow. Those who wait until these challenges have indeed become 'hot' issues are likely to fall behind, perhaps never to recover."
>
> *Peter Drucker*

A fundamental shift of attitude is therefore made clear.

R. HELLER

» *In Search of European Excellence* (HarperCollins Business, 1998)

Heller identifies a strategic approach to learning organizations as follows.

» Devolving leadership without losing control or direction.
» Driving radical change in the entire corporate system, as well as in its component parts.
» Reshaping and developing culture, attitudes, values and behavior and integrating these with long-term strategy, priority and direction.
» Dividing to rule, by which is meant the ability to respond to small opportunities whatever the size of the organization.
» Developing the central direction of the organization so that attitudes, behavior and economic realities are integrated.
» Maintaining competitive edge as a part of the development of organizations.
» Achieving constant renewal so that successes are part of a process, rather than causes for congratulation.

» Enhancing collective and individual motivation, and ensuring that people motivate themselves.
» Concentrating on high quality, high value and integrated teams.
» Paying attention to every part of each activity and process so that "total quality management" is achieved rather than aspired to.

This is achieved by accepting at first that there are certain to be corporate malaises, as follows.

» The organization and its top managers can do no wrong.
» The organization refuses to concede that mistakes have ever been made.
» Top management makes every decision regardless of knowledge and understanding of activities at the frontline.
» Top managers and others in positions of influence and power seek personal publicity and triumphs.
» Top managers and head offices monopolize power and influence at the expense of those with genuine knowledge and understanding.

Each of these elements requires a fundamental shift of attitude if organizations and their staff are to become fully effective and competitive. Alongside these shifts in top management, it is therefore required that skills, knowledge and expertise, as well as attitudes and behavior, are developed among all members of staff to ensure that opportunities can be responded to, and everything is conducted more effectively than in the past. Heller takes the view that, rather than being profligate with resources in attending to organization and employee development, resources are squandered through the centralization of power and physical distance of decision-making. By ensuring that everybody is developed to as high a level of expertise as possible, the waste that accrues from bad decision-making or expedient top management activity is to a large extent avoided.

C. ARGYRIS AND D.A. SCHON

» Argyris, C., **Personality and Organizations** (Harper & Row, 1957)
» Argyris, C. & Schon, D.A., **Organizational Learning** (Harper & Row, 1978)

Argyris and Schon identify seven dimensions along which the individual develops towards psychological maturity, as follows.

» Individuals move from passive states as infants to active states as adults.
» Individuals move from a state of dependency as infants to a state of relative independence as adults.
» Individuals have limited behavior as infants but complex and sophisticated behavior as adults.
» Individuals have short, casual and shallow interests as infants but deeper and stronger interests as adults.
» Infant's time spans and perspectives are very short; their concentration span is very short; with maturity this widens into conception of past and future.
» Infants are subordinate to others, and become peers, equals or superiors as adults.
» Infants lack self-awareness and self control; adults are self-aware and capable of self-control.

Argyris pursued this line of reasoning to the conclusion that highly structured and formalized organizations were therefore unsuitable places in which to work, especially for those who had a highly developed "adult." There is a fundamental lack of harmony or congruence between the needs of individuals and the drives and restraints of the organization. This tends to get worse as organizations become more sophisticated and rules, procedures and hierarchies grow, and also as individuals seek to progress themselves. This leads first to restriction, then frustration, and finally to conflict. Frustration and the potential for conflict are greatest at the lower levels of organizations where the ability to work independently is most restricted. The overall relationship is therefore fundamentally unsound and people are expected to behave in negative ways.

This caused Argyris (1957) and Argyris and Schon (1978) to consider the integrated development of organizations and individuals.

Single- and double-loop learning

Single-loop learning is identified as "the ability to know what to do in a particular set of circumstances, or as a response to specific triggers and stimuli." Individuals learn how they can do better, improving what they are currently doing. This may also be seen as learning at operational levels, or at the level of rules.

Double-loop learning is concerned with "why" in relation to what is being carried out. Lines of reasoning are added to the "what" approaches of single-loop learning so that, as well as learning new qualities and attributes, the "mental model" of reasoning, justification, evaluation and analysis is adjusted and developed also.

For double-loop learning to be effective, collective and corporate development is harmonized with individual enhancement. Attention is paid to fundamental principles, strategy and policies, organizational priorities, and hierarchies, ranks and reporting relationships because, as individual and collective capability advances, so do the institutions and structures of the organizations need to progress also.

P.M. SENGE

» *The Fifth Discipline* (Century Business, 1998)

Senge identifies the direct relationship between strategic, operational and productive success, and "the learning organization." The hypothesis is that organizations can succeed and prosper in the long term only if they are collectively, as well as individually, prepared to "learn faster than their competitors," and then apply the lessons learned in productive, effective and profitable ways. Senge identifies the following disciplines of the learning organization.

Systems thinking

Business and all human endeavors are systems. They are bound by invisible fabrics of interrelated actions that often take years to fully play out their effects on each other. Organizations traditionally tend to focus on events occurring in isolated parts of the system, rather than concentrating on the effectiveness of the whole. The ability to "think systematically" is conceptual rather than operational. It is necessary to develop bodies of knowledge and expertise around the way in which the whole works as well as each individual part. Thus, if attention is paid to one individual part, effects – including stresses and strains – on the rest of the whole will become apparent. In this way, organizations can *learn* to resolve problems from the point of view of reinvigorating the whole, rather than resolving them in the sure and certain knowledge that they will have knock-on effects leading to other issues.

Personal mastery

Personal mastery is the discipline of continually clarifying and deepening personal vision, focussing energy, as well as skills, qualities and expertise. Again, this reinforces the need for positive attitudes, values and behavior so that the context in which expertise is delivered sits comfortably with each individual who is required to work. Collectively and individually, it is necessary to clarify priorities and address these as the precursor to establishing the comfort and compatibility between organizations and those who work within them, and between organizations and their customers and clients. This form of comfort also reinforces mutual confidence and loyalty, as well as building a sound base for the development of expertise.

Mental models

Mental models are deeply ingrained assumptions, generalizations, pictures and images that influence how people understand the world and how they take action. These are forms of individual and collective perceptions that limit thinking and also skew or emphasize it in particular directions. There is a strong moral and economic element – what is required must serve individual and collective comfort and well-being, as well as economic demands. "Mental modeling" also includes the ability to identify and address preconceptions and prejudices and received wisdom, so that everything that is done is constantly a matter of scrutiny.

Building shared vision

Alongside the development of strategies, policies and priorities for action, "shared vision" is required – and this is closely related to culture, attitudes and values identification, development and transformation. Shared vision reinforces the need for strong and positive steps of dominant values to which everybody can aspire and with which they can be comfortable. Within this comfort is required the capacity for high levels of achievement and intrinsic recognition and reward, as well as attention again, to the wider social and moral issues – that the organization is "a good" place to work.

Team learning

Senge states

> "the discipline of team learning starts with dialogue; the capacity of members of a team to suspend assumptions and enter into genuine free thinking."

This underlines the value of communication, and the importance of developing mutual personal and professional respect and esteem, as well as high levels of performance. Those in different professions and occupations need to know how, and why, those in others operate and function as they do.

Conclusion

Learning organizations therefore concentrate on each of the foregoing elements. It requires acceptance that everyone, whatever their occupation, rank or level of experience is a learner. Attention is paid to each of the above elements, so that how particular and collective expertise may be applied is as important as what is required.

Senge proposes a strategic approach to organization and employee development based on the learning shortcomings of all organizations. The requirement is to understand that, in particular cases, it will be necessary to address specific issues; in the vast majority of cases, a collective strategic approach is required if each of these barriers is to be overcome. The approach adopted is functional, recognizing the need to develop from present starting points. The main tenets are as follows.

» Recognize the constraints of the present systems, and the sources of particular problems before trying to make fundamental and radical shifts.
» Recognize the allure – and the illusion – of short-term quick fixes rather than a strategic approach.

» Small changes can produce big results provided that they are fully integrated.
» Identify the blockages and see where the key interactions are causing problems; and recognize that dividing issues does not necessarily produce results – Heller uses the phrase "dividing an elephant in half does not produce two small elephants."
» Avoid apportioning blame – especially to those outside the organization, or to circumstances beyond control. This only works if it is fully integrated, and if there is a full acceptance of long-term enduring responsibility.

L. GRATTON

» *Living Strategy: Putting People at the Heart of Corporate Purpose* (Financial Times/Prentice Hall, 2000)

"People are our most important asset. We are a knowledge-based company. All we have is our people. These are statements we hear more and more. Yet, for many people, the reality of life in an organization is that they do not feel that they are treated as the most important asset, or that their knowledge is used or understood."

Gratton starts from that perspective, and develops the point further, indicating that there are fundamental differences, often resulting in conflicts, between what is required by the organization, and how they propose to implement it. She identifies four elements.

» There are fundamental differences between people as an asset, and the traditional assets of finance and technology.
» Understanding these fundamental differences creates the demand for whole new ways of thinking and working in organizations.
» Business strategies, policies and direction can only be realized through people.
» Creating strategic approaches to people necessitates a strong dialogue across all organizations.

It is essential, therefore, that people are put "at the heart of corporate purpose." This results in the creation of a "living strategy" – a following and fulfilling of corporate purpose and direction that is dependent upon individual and collective capability and willingness, and also on the required, desired and existing patterns of behavior among those carrying out the work.

Gratton identifies particularly "the soul of organizations." Based on work carried out at complex multinational organizations and public service bodies – including Hewlett Packard, Citibank and the UK's National Health Service, she identifies the subjective and emotional elements that people bring with them to work, and the extent to which these are satisfied (see Fig. 9.1).

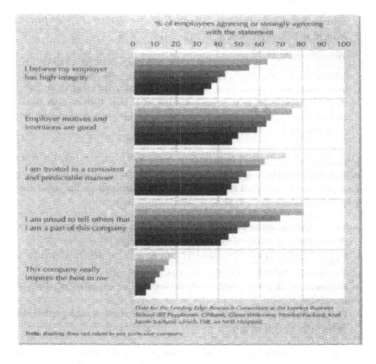

Fig. 9.1 The soul of the organization (Gratton, 2000, with permission).

This produces the capability to engage with "the soul of the organization," as follows:

» Create emotional capability through a range of measures which accurately reflect the emotional health of the organization.
» Build trust by removing unjust practices and replacing these with procedures and practices based on human, rather than procedural, elements.
» Construct a psychological contract based on the overriding mutuality of interest between individual and organization, and go on to generate identity, internalization and loyalty between both.

This is then to be integrated with the organization's purpose and direction as follows.

» Understand the short- and long-term goals of the organization.
» Understand the current and future capability requirements of the business to deliver to these goals, and have an awareness of gaps that exist, and the extent and prevalence of these.
» Design and implement "people processes" which are capable of changing the context in which people work, and which develop shared attitudes and values, and strong positive culture and "soul."

CONCLUSIONS

Each of these resources is a major contribution to the development of academic, operational and consultancy-based expertise. Each takes a distinctively different attitude and approach. However, the fundamental conclusion is very similar – in that it is impossible to generate effective sustainable organizational performance without paying attention to the needs and wants of people at work, and to creating the conditions in which their capabilities and willingness can be engaged and developed. There is a clear consensus that, whether OD is approached from the perspective of the understanding of culture, behavior, learning, or emotional commitment, investment is required in the human aspects of organizational life if they are to remain effective into the future.

FURTHER READING

Cartwright, R. (1994) *In Charge: Managing Yourself*. Blackwell.

Drucker, P. (1986) *The Effective Executive*. Fontana.

Hamel, G. (2000) *Leading the Revolution*. The Free Press.

Hammer, M. & Champy, J. (1994) *Re-engineering the Corporation*. Century Business.

Heller, R. (1998) *In Search of European Excellence*. HarperCollins.

Herzberg, F. (1960, 1987) *Work and the Nature of Man*. The Free Press.

Luthans, F. (1994) *Organizational Behaviour*. McGraw-Hill.

McCormack, M. (1982) *What They Don't Teach You at Harvard Business School*. Fontana.

Ohmae, K. (1996) *Work and Organization*. The Free Press.

Ouchi, W.G. (1981) *Theory Z*. Avon.

Peters, T. & Austin, N. (1986) *A Passion for Excellence: The Leadership Difference*. The Free Press.

Peters, T. & Waterman, R. (1982) *In Search of Excellence*. Harper & Row.

Pettinger, R. (1996) *Introduction to Organizational Behaviour*. Macmillan.

– (2000) *Mastering Organizational Behaviour*. Macmillan Palgrave.

– (2001) *Mastering Management Skills*. Macmillan Palgrave.

Porter, M.E. (1980) *Competitive Strategy*. The Free Press.

– (1985) *Competitive Advantage*. The Free Press.

Sternberg, E. (1995) *Just Business*. Warner.

Semler, R. (1992) *Maverick*. The Free Press.

Wickens, P. (1992) *The Road to Nissan*. Collins.

– (1998) *The Ascendent Organization*. Collins.

Woodward, J. (1970) *Industrial Organization: Behaviour and Control*. Oxford University Press.

Ten Steps to Making Learning Organizations Work

The 10 steps to a successful learning organization are in summary:

1 Resources
2 Induction and orientation
3 Attitudes to success and failure
4 Problem-solving
5 Project work
6 Employability
7 Understanding how and why people learn
8 The whole person and the organization
9 Human capital
10 Corporate attitudes and management style.

The key to successful implementation of learning organization strategies is to ensure that the human side of enterprise and aspects of performance are fully understood in the context required. Organization capability has to be matched with product and service requirements in terms of creating the conditions, establishing culture, collective attitudes and shared values, and attending to absolute standards of behavior as well as performance. Unless this is understood, the effectiveness of the approach is sure to be limited.

1. RESOURCES

Capital resources are required to ensure that the desired technology and equipment is available, and for the development of the expertise necessary to maximize and optimize long-term returns (see Summary box 10.1).

SUMMARY BOX 10.1: RESOURCES AND EQUIPMENT

The standard priority is to ensure that state-of-the-art equipment is available rather than expertise and commitment. Learning organizations require the reverse. This was expressed by Tom Peters, in a Channel 4 television program, *The World Turned Upside Down* in 1986, as follows:

> "When I went to a Nissan truck plant at Smyrna, Tennessee, I was not impressed by their technology. I had seen better in Detroit. What did impress me was the $12,000 per head spent on training before the production lines were switched on. I am the biggest fan of reliability data coming out of Detroit and it's real simple – American cars don't work! There is not a trade barrier high enough to save us from our own folly in this."

Nissan had based their ability to gain competitive advantage by ensuring that adequate technology was available and staff were fully trained, rather than relying on superior equipment with an under-trained workforce.

This includes commitment to the development of expertise in mentoring, coaching and counseling, and core and on-the-job training activities. Space and time require inclusion to ensure that those activities undertaken as projects by individuals and groups can be brought to fruition, as well as ensuring that the capacity exists for people to engage in effective and supported general development activities. Where deadlines are tight, this either means starting earlier or arranging flexibility so that late and overnight working can be engaged (where necessary), but not abused.

Resource allocation includes the identification of development responsibilities for all, and this includes senior and executive staff. Their time priorities, and general standards of attitude and behavior, require allocating and enforcing so that they also participate when required.

2. INDUCTION AND ORIENTATION

Induction and orientation are absolute requirements in terms of ensuring that those who come into the organization quickly learn the ways in which they are required to deliver their expertise, as well as developing it further.

This is clearly understood by Japanese manufacturing organizations (see Summary box 10.1 and Chapters 3, 4 and 7). The lessons that must be learned are:

» the necessity of doing this early so that preconceptions and misunderstandings are kept to a minimum alongside developing the required attitudes and values;
» the necessity to view it as a priority whatever conflicting work pressures may be present; and
» the necessity to commit staff and other resources to ensure continued high quality.

The induction balance must be recognized (see Fig. 10.1). The priority here is attitudes and behavior, rather than skills and knowledge – because it is essential to gain staff commitment leading to loyalty and identity as a precursor to being effective in the job.

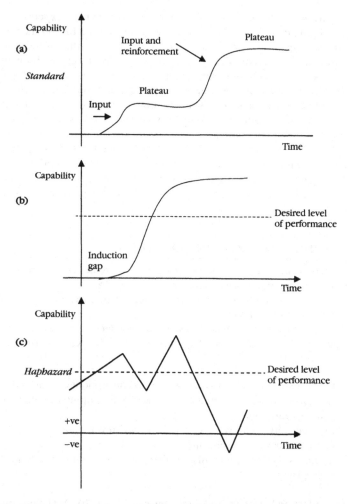

Fig. 10.1 Learning curves. (a) Theoretical – based on rational and ordered input, familiarization, practice and reinforcement. (b) The theory of induction–time taken at the outset leads to long-term high levels of performance. (c) The theory of non-induction and non-training – based on trial and error.

3. ATTITUDES TO ACHIEVEMENT

Attitudes to achievement must be based on the following.

» Why and how are aims and objectives set, and how are they to be measured, when, where and by whom (and this includes customers and clients)?
» There must be a broader conception ensuring that lessons are learned along the way from everything that is undertaken.
» There has to be a capability and willingness to distinguish between shortcomings as the result of negligence and incompetence, and other causes. This leads to the complete abolition of any culture of blame (negligence and incompetence are dealt with through disciplinary and poor-performance procedures).
» There has to be a strategic approach to designing and implementing clear standards of what is rewarded, and what is not; and what is punished, and what is not (see Summary box 10.2).

SUMMARY BOX 10.2: REWARDS AND PUNISHMENTS

Individuals need to be aware of this because rewards and punishments underline actual (as distinct from stated) organizational attitudes. The requirements are clarity and integrity, so that:

» genuine mistakes and shortcomings are evaluated and learned from rather than punished;
» rewards are given for achievement rather than compliance with procedures;
» deviations in standards of behavior (especially bullying, victimization, violence, harassment and discrimination) are punished by dismissal where proven; and
» there is a fundamental equality of approach which means that the bases for reward and punishment are the same for everyone regardless of rank, status, occupation or length of service.

4. PROBLEM-SOLVING

Effective approaches recognize the certainty of problems occurring and embrace them as individual and collective learning opportunities. Problems may be referred to work improvement groups, quality improvement groups and quality circles, as well as to brainstorming sessions. More serious issues may become substantial group and individual projects. The key requirement is attitude and approach, so that both time and resources may be made available even where a quick solution to a particular issue is required.

Underpinning this is a corporate attitude that taking time and trouble to develop problem-solving capabilities means that a greater range of expertise is available so that matters are raised and recognized early, and actions to resolve them can then be taken quickly. Moreover, involving staff directly in these activities means that they are much more likely to learn the lessons required, and to ensure that if similar things do arise again they are dealt with quickly and effectively (see Summary box 10.3).

SUMMARY BOX 10.3: MATSUSHITA

Matsushita, the Japanese electrical goods giant, had just won planning approval to extend and enlarge one of its factory sites in the UK. This was going to lead to the creation of 1,400 new jobs. The company had initially got itself into difficulties by underestimating the size and nature of the working environment that it was going to require if its local activity was to be fully effective. The local chief executive was asked the following.

» *Interviewer*: So then – you don't make mistakes. You get everything right first time, every time?
» *Response*: Of course we make mistakes. I make them – lots of them – everyday. Look at the present situation – we could have got ourselves into all sorts of difficulties with this situation. Now we have realized our mistake, we will put it right. The important thing – the reason why the company is so successful – is that when we make mistakes, we acknowledge them, and learn from them.

5. PROJECT WORK

The ability to pursue project work as a part of individual and collective development is required. This means allocating both capacity and resources to allow groups and individuals to get involved in areas of personal, professional, occupational, technological and organizational interest, provided that it does not dilute their core effort and primary responsibilities. This requires a corporate attitude that recognizes the following:

» the precise value of such work as a contribution to the future performance of the organization, as well as the actual outputs of the project in hand; and
» the derived value in terms of developing staff loyalty and commitment, as well as all round capability.

It does not mean satisfying and supporting every whim and interest brought to the organization's attention by individuals. It does mean evaluating each proposal on its merits, and agreeing a remit, terms of reference, reporting relations and points of contact (including supervision, mentoring and guidance) so that what is produced satisfies either the primary or derived value, or both.

Sources of project work include the following:

» suggestion schemes;
» off-the-job course content in which, in many cases, project work is required as a condition of completing the course;
» problem-solving activities;
» technology development and introduction;
» macro issues such as product potential or market analysis; and
» feasibility studies, and product and service piloting and testing.

Whatever the source, the project approach requires being made available to all and positive encouragement for everyone undertaking this form of work. It also requires a fundamentally equal intrinsic value whatever the level of project activity carried out, and whether it is addressing a large or very small issue.

6. EMPLOYABILITY

Learning organizations develop individual and collective employability (see Chapter 3) through attending to the following.

» *Capability* – professional, occupational and job skills, knowledge, expertise and technical development.
» *Individual and collective willingness, commitment and motivation* – through the development of required attitudes and values.
» *Creativity* – as the result of engaging the active interest of everyone involved in projects and problem-solving.
» *Potential* – as the result of giving people opportunities that they would otherwise not have.

There are conditions attached. Reward levels must be high enough to meet the desired aim of high-quality work and high-level capability. New skills, knowledge and expertise must be built on further and developed through the ability to practice. Those carrying out overtly mundane work must be encouraged and supported when they find other opportunities. Failure to address each of these points leads to heightened levels of frustration, and those who are able to do so find jobs at other organizations.

It may also have to be accepted that it is only possible to retain some staff for limited periods before they do move on. In these cases, the drive is to get as much from them as possible before they do go on without compromising the overall approach. This tends to enhance general organizational reputation for high-quality employment practices. It enhances attractiveness to the next generation of employees. It also tends to encourage more general reputation, and generates high levels of favorable responses among communities in which the organization is located.

7. UNDERSTANDING HOW AND WHY PEOPLE LEARN

The foregoing reinforces the need for effective time management and resource allocation. People are prepared and willing to learn:

» if it is in their own intrinsic or extrinsic interests; and /or
» if they are to be rewarded in some way (e.g. enhanced pay and opportunities at work, personal preference away from work).

Learning is reinforced through the capacity to practice under guidance and then to accept responsibility. Continuous feedback is required, and this is a key role of mentors, supervisors and those with greater expertise. Organization conditions require that this be given in constructive and non-punitive ways to reinforce what is done well and address gaps so that these can be remedied. In his book *Experience as the Source of Learning and Development* (Prentice Hall, 1985), Kolb proposed a learning cycle as shown in Fig. 10.2.

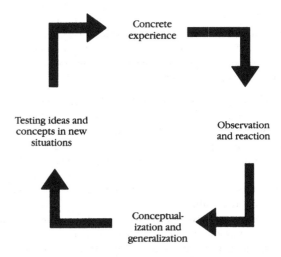

Fig. 10.2 Learning cycle. The cycle illustrates the importance of the relationship between behavior, action and experience. It also emphasizes (testing and experience) the need to reinforce abstract learning with practice and performance (Kolb, 1985, with permission).

Especial attention is required to reinforcing the testing of ideas and concepts in new situations, and on the capacity for observation and reflection. In general, reinforcement may be:

» continuous, in which case the learning is soon internalized;
» intermittent, in which case it is likely to become important from time to time only, and may lead to the need for revision, retraining and refresher courses; or

» occasional, in which case the learning is likely to have been of general or marginal value only.

Feedback and reinforcement are essential on all aspects of performance leading to enhanced levels of understanding, confidence, capability and support, and reinforcing attitudes and values. It is best in the following circumstances:

» when it is positive rather than negative, enhancing the general concept of progress, as well as specific advances; and
» when it concentrates on processes, as well as results, so that individuals both know how they have got on, and also understand why they have succeeded or failed.

Reinforcement, retention and feedback activities are best delivered as near to the conclusion of the learning as possible and then followed up with opportunities to apply that which has been learned. This should then be incorporated into longer range feedback processes, and formally commented on at regular performance reviews.

This is further enhanced by visibility and accessibility between staff, managers and supervisors. The effect is diluted when managers and supervisors are not visible.

This enhances and develops motivation and commitment to learn. It also means that induction and other learning curves are sustained and reinforced, rather than allowed to emerge piecemeal (see Fig. 10.1).

8. THE WHOLE PERSON AND THE ORGANIZATION

Organization development attends to all aspects of behavior, attitude, skills, knowledge, expertise and technological enhancement. It attends to these from the point of view of ensuring personal, as well as organizational, occupational and professional development. Each feeds of the others. For example, development of IT proficiency reinforces personal and occupational confidence; supporting people when they learn non-work skills (e.g. cookery, foreign languages) reinforces feelings of mutual loyalty and identity.

The greater the all-round development, the higher the total value of the employee and their expertise. The following points should be noted.

» Those who concentrate only on organizational requirements become narrow and constrained.

» Those who concentrate on occupational development miss opportunities and potential elsewhere.

» For those with professional qualifications (e.g. medicine, law, accountancy, engineering) who concentrate only on their professional development, the organization is effectively sponsoring career paths in which organizational advantage is merely a by-product.

» Those who use organizational largesse to pursue personal interests to the exclusion of all else may be retained in the short to medium term; however, the organization is being sold short on its part of the bargain. Also, those employees who do pursue personal interests from this point of view fully understand that they are taking advantage of the particular situation, and so they themselves contaminate the relationship.

A fully comprehensive joint venture is therefore required so that each element is as fully developed as possible.

9. HUMAN CAPITAL

Attending to employability, and how and why people learn, gives the best possible chance of developing "human capital" or knowledge and expertise management and development. The ability to recruit, develop and retain those with high quality and required expertise is a major current organizational and managerial priority. Those who have demonstrated and proven track records, and reputation for producing results, are themselves highly marketable commodities.

Human asset valuation

Approaches to valuing human assets and expertise have been attempted by organizations and individuals. This is straightforward where there is effectively a commodity trade taking place (see Summary box 10.2). It is harder, and some would say less wholesome and ethical, when it is attempted in general terms. The approach normally adopted is to assume a pragmatic view in which staff capabilities and expertise are assessed in terms of costs and benefits, or balancing what they contribute with what they cost.

Returns may be measured and assessed in the same way as for any other asset; and, above all, provide information for managerial discussion. Additional factors have to be taken into account however. These are:

» the opportunity costs of the current human resource;
» measures of goodwill;
» the balance and mix of talents and capacities with operational requirements; and
» current and projected asset values for each occupational group.

If this approach is taken, it is essential to address the aspects of "human liability." This means assessing any actual or projected occupational obsolescence or decline, and consequent depreciation of the asset. A full staffing obligation and responsibility, as well as narrow occupational liability, replacement costs, and "refurbishment" (retraining, redeployment and redevelopment) costs must also be considered.

This is all based on employment costs. A fully integrated approach requires that these be included in the fixed cost base of the organization. It is also possible to establish these by: staff category; department, division or function; the added value contributed by each occupation, job and profession; and through the consideration of local and sectoral factors, including the requirement to pay high levels of wages in areas and locations where staff are scarce.

This can be modeled as shown in Fig. 10.3.

In organizations where there is a genuine commitment to the human side of enterprise, there is normally a strong conflict present between

» the reality of looking at staff as an asset to be maximized and optimized over the long term, and
» the moral question of viewing people in this way as commodities.

There is nothing wrong with the approach provided that the organization clearly understands the standpoint adopted, and the ethical dispositions that go with it. Failure to do so is normally a function of remote hierarchical, bureaucratic and administration-oriented management; and in these circumstances, learning organization strategies are unlikely to be present anyway.

1. THE BASE

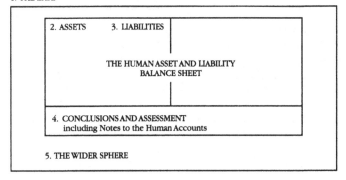

Fig. 10.3 The context of human asset valuation.

10. CORPORATE ATTITUDES AND MANAGEMENT STYLE

The linchpin of effective long-term learning organization strategies, and accrued successful and profitable performance, are the collective attitudes and style adopted. These require the following:

» high levels of moral integrity based on openness and mutuality of interest, trust and commitment;
» receptiveness to new ideas and approaches from whatever the source;
» the prioritization of managerial and supervisory tasks and key result areas to accommodate the need to develop staff; and
» the development of the skills, qualities and expertise of assessment, appraisal, mentoring, coaching, counseling and tutoring; of evaluation and review; and of high individual levels of openness and integrity.

Also required in many cases, especially where these approaches are engaged as change management strategies, is the radical shift of perception away from the restrictions, ranks and roles of traditional and enduring organizational approaches (see Summary box 10.4).

SUMMARY BOX 10.4: PERCEPTIONS

Two extreme managerial perceptions may be identified.

1 Expert staff are a threat and a reflection of the manager's own inadequacies, and lack of capability and expertise, in some areas. Where present, this must be acknowledged. Where necessary, steps must be taken to overcome this. Such attitudes may have arisen as the result of malice. It is far more likely that they are based on fear and ignorance. Managers and supervisors placed in these positions must be given support as they develop the new required capabilities and attitudes so that progress is made towards the following other extreme.

2 Managers adopt the view that long-term effective and profitable work is possible only with high-quality, expert and committed staff. Many of these will inevitably know more about the particular tasks and activities than the manager involved. Managers and supervisors who adopt this stance find their positions reinforced rather than threatened. This also underlines the increasingly accepted position that management is a trade and expertise in its own right; and that it has its own set of responsibilities and priorities, rather than being threatened by the capabilities and expertise of those in non-managerial professions and occupations.

CONCLUSIONS

As stated at the outset (see Chapter 1), learning organizations require long-term and strategic commitments to securing high levels of capability, motivation, output, and effective and profitable organizational performance. Addressing each of the above ten steps indicates the level of commitment required. It indicates where potential barriers and blockages to progress may exist. Organizations and managers who are thinking of pursuing these strategies need to be able to assess each honestly and openly so that the extent and scale of practical problems that may be present are understood at the outset.

It is also necessary to be able to demonstrate these steps (or their equivalent) to backers and shareholders' representatives. The results of the approach are likely not to become apparent in the short term. Liaison with, and management of, these groups is required to ensure that their commitment is not lost or called into question. All achievements should be presented and communicated from the point of view of harmonizing the effectiveness of this approach to organization management with the long-term demands of backers.

KEY LEARNING POINTS

» There is a relationship between learning and development, and organizational business success.
» Specific areas of intervention are important – induction, attitudes to success and failure, and effectiveness in problem-solving activities.
» The contributions of all activities to individual and collective development must be recognized.
» There is a moral and ethical commitment required to collective and individual employability, and to all aspects of development – personal, occupational, organizational and professional.
» It is essential to understand how and why people learn, and how this is reinforced and made effective.
» It is necessary to recognize the organizational, financial and moral aspects of placing value (and therefore, inevitably, price) on staff, expertise and capabilities.
» It is important to understand the prioritization of learning and development activities in managerial and supervisory tasks and patterns of work.
» It is also important to recognize the value of prioritizing learning and development activities in the workload of all staff.

Frequently Asked Questions (FAQs)

Q1: What exactly are "learning organizations?"

A: Refer to Chapters 2 and 6.

Q2: Why do I/we need to know anything about it?

A: Refer to Chapters 3 and 10.

Q3: How do we measure the returns on our investment?

A: Refer to Chapters 6, 7 and 10.

Q4: How do we convince our shareholders and other stakeholders?

A: Refer to Chapters 3, 4 and 5.

Q5: How do we keep it going once we have got it under way?

A: Refer to Chapters 7, 9 and 10.

Q6: What happens if the senior managers wish to change direction?

A: Refer to Chapters 6, 7 and 10.

Q7: Is this all a bit soft – why should we be involved in training and development?

A: Refer to Chapters 3, 6, 7 and 10.

Q8: If we train the staff, will they not leave?

A: Refer to Chapters 7 and 10.

Q9: How does it work in relation to TQM, BPR and other consultancy-led initiatives?

A: Refer to Chapters 3–6 and 10.

Q10: How much does it cost?

A: Refer to Chapters 7 and 10.

Index

Printed in the United States
By Bookmasters